Piccolo Eating Book

Fabulous and Funny Food Facts

Bronwen O'Connor

Piccolo eating book

Fabulous and funny food facts

Illustrated by Nick Price

A Piccolo original
Pan Books London and Sydney

First published 1976 by Pan Books Ltd,
Cavaye Place, London SW10 9PG
© Bronwen O'Connor 1976
ISBN 0 330 24562 7
Printed and bound in Great Britain by
Richard Clay (The Chaucer Press) Ltd, Bungay, Suffolk

To my mother and Deryn, two good cooks

✳ Special offer
To readers of this book

King Alfred's burnt-cake mix

The secret of success in making these cakes is Not To Worry. Just add water to the cake mix. Heat the oven in someone else's cottage. Pop the cakes in, and then you can *forget all about them*. You can easily tell when the cakes are done – smoke will be coming out of the door.

Marie Antoinette's
let-them-eat-cake recipe

Take two whipped peasants and bind them. Beat well. Put them under the guillotine for a few seconds. When the peasants rise, you can either serve them straightaway – or run. Offer closes 1789.

Just send us a packet and your name and address. Allow some time for delivery.

Read all about it!
Man eats frogs

Mr John McNamara, aged forty-two, of County Clare, ate five live frogs in sixty-five seconds to become the All-Ireland Live-Frog Swallowing Champion. One of his five opponents was disqualified for chewing.

Dog eats man

There was a young man from Bengal,
Who went to a fancy-dress ball.
 He thought he would risk it,
 And went as a biscuit,
But a dog ate him up, in the hall.

Dog eats hat

One day, a little man was walking along the road when a big dog ran after him, jumped up, knocked off his hat, and chewed it up. The dog then ran off down the road and disappeared into a front garden. The little man walked up to the door of the house and knocked. A big man opened it and said, gruffly, 'What do you want?'

'Your dog has just chewed up my hat,' said the little man.

'So what?' said the big man, and slammed the door.

The little man plucked up his courage and knocked on the door again.

'Well?' said the big man, in the doorway.

'I don't like your attitude,' said the little man, bravely.

'It's not *my* 'at 'e chewed,' said the big man, 'it's *your* 'at 'e chewed.'

Sam Stubbins's celebrated free food lecture 1

Given in the village hall of Little Nibbling
(Actually, this isn't the first lecture Sam's given. He did give one before, but there was an entrance fee of 2p – children half-price. The trouble was, Sam found it a bit lonely, talking to himself all evening. So after that he reduced the entrance fee by 2p. Steve Jones, who's a crafty beggar, said, 'In that case you owe me a penny.' But Sam wasn't having any of *that* kind of nonsense.)

The mystery of the plastic bag

Sam Stubbins, Celebrated Food Lecturer, stood on the platform, turning out his overcoat pockets. That took quite a time.

He unloaded a ball of string, a milk bottle, three large plastic bags, one chicken (dead), a detergent bottle, two left-hand socks and a balaclava helmet. The rest of his pockets he just looked into, shaking his head sadly.

'Blast it,' he said, 'I've lost me notes. All about the invention of cooking, too. I had a good lecture there. Well, never mind, everyone knows how cooking started. That was when we lost the hair off the bottom of our feet, of course.'

Sam looked down at his feet. Sure enough, there was no hair on them. There were no shoes or socks, either. He went on with the lecture, putting on the two left-hand socks at the same time.

'There was this clumsy caveman who came home with a rabbit, tripped over the doormat at the front of the cave, stumbled into the fire, dropped the rabbit into the hot ashes, hopped out yelling blue murder, poked the rabbit out with a long stick – result: **roast rabbit**. The **invention of cooking**. It was an amazing feat, really.'

Sam looked down at his. "Course, if asbestos shoes hadn't gone out of fashion the year before, he'd have kept his hair on – but you can't have everything. And, as you know, the invention of cooking led to many others – such as **electricity** to heat the micro-wave ovens, and **walls** to plug the electricity into, and then **roofs** to keep the switches dry, which led to the invention of **houses**. Then, all the food in shopping-baskets looked kind of silly sitting in the back seat of nothing, so they had to invent **motor-cars** to fit round them. 'Course, the **kitchen sink** came next, when some bloke began wondering why all the plates and water kept smashing and splashing on the floor when he was washing-up . . .'

'Are you kidding?' asked Bert Jenkins.

''Course I am,' said Sam. 'But I'll tell you something that's being invented right now – and that's food.'

'But food just *is*,' said Minty Jenkins. 'You don't have to invent it.'

'Wrong and double wrong,' said Sam. 'You thinking about cows in green fields and all that sort of thing?'

'I suppose so,' said Minty.

'Well, I'm thinking about this,' said Sam, throwing a handful of coins on to the table. (One fell on to the floor, and Steve Jones made a mental note of where it was, for afterwards.) 'Money. That's the mother of invention, money is. Now, you've got one field. You put a cow in it. That's food for ten people for a month, say? Now, you grow soya beans in that field, and you get food for *seventy* people for a month. So, it stands to reason, with land getting less and people

getting more, you don't grow cows, you grow soya beans. 'Course, if you're growing wheat, then you grow this instead.'

He pulled a head of corn out of his top right-hand pocket.

'This is the Green Revolution. Heard of it? It's wheat that grows two, three times bigger and better than wheat used to be. Discovered by the Americans. They grow it all over the world, now. But, supposing you still want your chickens and your cows and your pigs. Then you invent this . . .' He delved into his inside bottom pocket and brought out a plastic-wrapped chicken. 'Know what this is?'

'That's an oven-ready chicken,' said Mollie Pratt.

'That's Agribusiness,' said Sam, 'begging your pardon. In the old days, there used to be Agriculture *and* Business. *Now*, you put your cow in a cell, and your chicken on to a shelf. You don't let them roam around. That's wasteful. Uses up energy and space. So you shut them up – that's Agribusiness, or Factory Farming, one of the Food Inventions. 'Course, you can be a bit *too* clever. Like the Professor of Bird Genetics who developed two hundred *bald* chickens. They was your genuine, walking, oven-ready chicks. Trouble was, they got colds and ulcers, and didn't lay so many eggs.'

'But they still have to grow *some* things in fields, surely?' said Colonel Chumley-Mutt. 'I mean to say, I've got an orchard. You couldn't grow apples in sheds, now could you? I mean to say, what?'

'You still got an orchard?' asked Sam. 'With big trees, what you have to reach up to and pick?'

'Of course,' said the Colonel, rather huffily. 'And damned good apples they are, too.'

'Well, it takes all sorts,' said Sam. ''Course, the new thing is mini-orchards. You sprays your tree when it's about two foot high, with a chemical what stops it growing. Then you just get a machine what whips along the line, picking the apples. The next year you cuts it down to the ground and starts again. Oranges now – there's a machine with six large blowers that blasts air into the trees. Down tumble the oranges into a catching net. That's orange-picking for you. 'Course, there again, you can be a bit too clever. There was a machine invented for harvesting lettuces. It's so efficient – picks four rows at a time – that six hundred of those would harvest all the lettuces in the world. Now, that's a bit much. I mean, what about all the lettuce-pickers in the world? So it never got put into production.'

'Mr Stubbins,' said Mrs Prendergast.

'Yes?' said Sam.

'Mr Stubbins,' said Mrs Prendergast again, earnestly, 'what's all this nowadays about beef being made out of beans, or some such nonsense?'

'Ah, that's good stuff,' said Sam. 'You interested in sewing, Mrs P.?'

'Well . . . I do a bit now and then . . .'

'Well, here's a fine bit of material,' said Sam, holding up a beef-burger. 'Spun protein, you know. Fascinating business. You put your soya bean into a vat of alkali. Then you squeeze it through little holes, and you get fibres, like cotton. Then you give a bit of a stretch here, and a pull there, you wind it into a hank, you press it and cut it – and there you are – Meat Analogue. That's another name for it – 'course, that's quite old-fashioned now.'

'What do you mean, old-fashioned?' said Bert. 'Isn't that bad enough?'

'It isn't *bad*,' said Sam. 'It's good food. Soya's good protein. Trouble is, you've got to use land to grow it on. So now, they're working on growing plants without earth. There's progress for you. You just grow them in water. Grow them anywhere, in green-houses. Hydroponics, they call it. Take waste, now. They're work-ing on that, too. Making food out of leftovers from paper-making, and waste from petrol-refining. Old paper. Take this,' he went on, holding up the plastic bag. 'That's food, if you did but know it.'

'You mean we're going to eat *those*?' said Mrs Prendergast, in horror.

'Hold your horses, Mrs P.,' said Sam soothingly. 'Not exactly, no. What they do is, they grow simple organisms, microscopic little things, in huge vats of this waste stuff. Why, overnight you could grow the equivalent of half a cow in one large tank of petro-chemicals. Protein, that is – not your actual hoofer. What a saving. That really puts your cow back in the Dark Ages.'

'But . . .' said Minty slowly. 'Suppose you don't have any more cows, then what about milk?'

'Oh well,' said Sam, 'that's it, isn't it? I mean, we'll just have to do without. Here, have a drop.'

He handed down the milk bottle to Minty. 'The End of the World is at hand,' he announced. 'Have a swig while it's still about.'

Minty took a mouthful, just to please Sam.

'OK?' asked Sam.

'All right,' said Minty. 'Not very creamy, though.'

'Not bad, though, considering it's made of mashed green-pea pods and cabbage leaves, eh? That's Plantmilk. Just another Food Invention.'

Minty was sitting rather stunned. She gave the milk a sniff.

'But how do they get the right taste? I don't see.'

'I'll tell you later,' said Sam. 'See you next week, and I'll let you into the Secret of the Rancid Water-Buffalo.'

'But what's that got to do with this milk?' asked Minty.

'Wait and see,' said Sam.

Useful recipes
from famous people 1

Here's one from **Sir John Betjeman,** the poet

'All I know about cooking is how to boil an egg, and I can give you the recipe for this. Take a saucepan and fill it with water, warm if possible so that it does not take quite so long to come to the boil as it would if it were cold. Now get an egg, preferably a fresh one, and put it into the water, at the same time trying to avoid scalding your fingers. I forgot to say that the water must be boiling before you insert the egg. One way I have found of putting in the egg without burning my fingers and cracking the shell is to put it in with a spoon. Leave it in the boiling water for a few minutes. You can never tell whether it's going to be too soft or too hard. That is one of the many mysteries of cooking.'

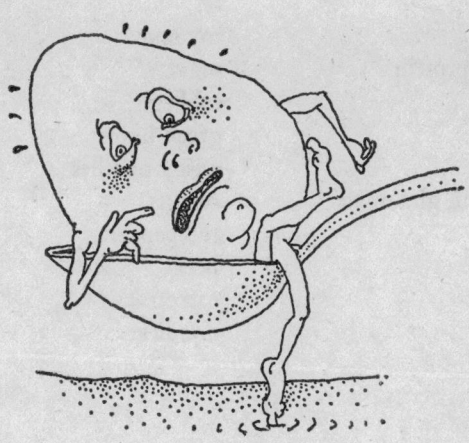

Watch it, folks!

Did you know?

That nearly all tins and packets and jars of food have a list of ingredients somewhere on them? Usually, they are hidden away in very small print.

Did you know?

That these must by law be printed in a special order? The two lists below both show what goes into a packet of Dried Beef Noodles. One of them really is what is on the packet. The other would be completely disgusting. Which is which?

noodles	antioxidant
carrots	colouring
beef	preservative
red peppers	flavouring
onions	monosodium glutamate
crispy noodles	parsley
green beans	farina
cabbage	salt
sugar	hydrolized protein
soy sauce	fat
fat	soy sauce
hydrolized protein	sugar
salt	cabbage
farina	green beans
parsley	crispy noodles
monosodium glutamate	onions
flavouring	red peppers
preservative	beef
colouring	carrots
antioxidant	noodles

The one on the left is the real list. The ingredients have to be listed in order of *amount*. So, there are more noodles than anything else, then carrots, right down to antioxidant. If you could buy something made out of the right-hand list, then you'd probably need a microscope to see the noodles!

Do you know what you're eating?

Guess what?
A packet of what food has this list of ingredients?

beef	sodium polyphosphates
onions	hydrolized vegetable protein
soya flour	monosodium glutamate
wheat flour	spice extract
rusk	onion extract
salt	

A packet of beef burgers

A jar of what food has this list of ingredients on the label?

vegetable oil	mustard
vinegar	gum carob
sugar	lactic acid
eggs	herbs
salt	vegetable colouring

A jar of Heinz salad cream

And what has this list on its paper wrapper?

sugar	sodium citrate
glucose syrup	flavouring
stabilizer	calcium carbonate
fruit acid	saccharine
calcium acid phosphate	colouring

Sky-ray ice lolly

The case of the missing ingredient

In Cadbury's *chicken*-flavoured soup mix the main ingredients are: glucose syrup solids, potato starch, vegetable fat, edible starch, salt and chicken-flavoured powder – but no chicken as such!

When did they start?

Tinned food

A Frenchman called Louis Alpert began tinning vegetables in 1810. By the 1860s they were tinning meat – corned beef.

Captain Scott's expedition to the South Pole in 1912 left behind stores of unopened tins of food in the snow. They were opened about fifty years later, and the food was perfectly all right.

✳ You name it – there's a tin of it somewhere. There's a tinning factory in Whale Cove, in Hudson Bay, which tins food for the Eskimos. You can get whale in gravy, whalemeat balls, *muklik* (the skin of the white whale), sealmeat balls, seal liver in gravy and seal flipper.

Frozen food

People have kept food fresh with ice for centuries. Big houses used to have their own ice-houses, filled with huge chunks of ice bought by the load.

Francis Bacon, the seventeenth-century writer, caught pneumonia and died – all because he jumped out of his carriage one day in the snow, and started stuffing a chicken with it. He wondered if that

would preserve it. (History doesn't record what happened to the chicken.)

But *freezing*, instead of just keeping cold, was the invention of a Mr Clarence Birdseye. One day, he was on a visit to Labrador, up in the coldest parts of Canada. He saw fish lying about, frozen stiff by the Arctic temperature. That was it. He got the idea. He set up the first frozen food factory in New York, in July 1923.

✳ There's a frozen food storage plant in Illinois that only deals in baked goods. It's entirely computer-controlled and deals with *eight million* cakes at one time.

At the moment, though, ordinary people have to go to a shop, pick out the food, and bring it home in baskets. All very primitive. In the future, we may drive into a large central yard and buy a container filled with a whole season's supply of food. You'd go shopping about three or four times a year.

Moonfood
No one will ever live *on* the moon – that's most unlikely. But they may live *in* the moon, deep under the surface. On the moon, the day lasts for two weeks, and the temperature can reach boiling point. In the two-week night, the temperature can drop to minus 150° centigrade. But man, living under the surface, wouldn't be exposed to all that. So moon colonies could live there.

What about food? First of all, man will take his own. But that won't last for ever. And, as far as we know, there is neither oxygen nor water on the moon, though there could be some water deep inside. And these are all necessary for the growing of food. But they can be got – from recycling human waste, and the waste from the first supplies taken from the earth. Carbon dioxide breathed out by the moon settlers can be converted to oxygen and carbon. Hydrogen is one of the commonest elements in the universe. Out of the hydrogen and oxygen, water can be made. And from human waste, you can get nitrogen, phosphorus and minerals which would help the plants to grow.

So what will the moonmen grow? It will have to be micro-organisms, minute plants which will be grown on the waste materials, as is now being done on earth. That will be the diet in the beginning. Anything else, like chickens or rabbits, would be too wasteful, using up more materials than they produce. But it could be that when the moon colony gets going, producing enough algae, or micro-organisms, then there could be the odd chicken kept. Now, if they could discover how to make food out of water, carbon dioxide and waste materials, by some chemical process, that would save all the trouble of growing the plants . . .

On one space mission – Gemini 12 – astronauts Lovell and Aldrich each ate in one day:

shrimp cocktail	pineapple fruit cake
chicken in gravy	coconut cubes
toasted bread cubes	orange-grapefruit drink

But you can't *pour* anything out, or put it on a plate, or use a spoon, in a rocket – because everything would be all over the place, due to weightlessness. You'd get shrimp cocktail right in the eye. So, all the food is *dehydrated* – dried out completely – and kept in containers. Then, through a nozzle, you can add water, and eat the mixture direct from the container.

Food quiz 1
Guess when?

Here is a description of an intensive farm unit for rearing birds and animals.

The farm is carefully geared to rear and fatten mostly small animals and birds. This is because of the expense of raising large animals, and because they take up too much valuable land if put out into the fields. But there are salt- and fresh-water ponds, stocked with all kinds of fish. Pigeon houses and aviaries are dimly lit, and are packed with quail, ortolans, thrushes and blackbirds to be fattened for the table. The young pigeons are left in their nests, but their legs are broken so they can't fly away. There is a special house for guinea-fowl, which are considered a special treat by some people. Two hundred birds are kept in two houses, each of which is $1\frac{1}{2}$ metres $\times$ 3 metres (5 ft $\times$ 10 ft), and $1\frac{1}{2}$ metres (5 ft) high. The ordinary poultry are kept in darkened hen coops, with the feathers pulled out of the wings and tails. Dormice and guinea-pigs are also kept on the farm. They are brought indoors and fattened in darkened jars.

Is this happening:
120 years ago in the eastern parts of Russia?
1,800 years ago in Italy?
A short while ago in certain parts of Asia?
On a factory farm in Norfolk today?
At some imaginary time in the future?

(Answer on page 153)

Guess what?

What food or drink are these places famous for?

1 Frankfurt	10 Edinburgh
2 Champagne	11 Caerphilly
3 Dundee	12 Oporto
4 Gloucester	13 Alaska
5 Worcester	14 Banbury
6 Jerusalem	15 Cheddar
7 Seville	16 New Zealand
8 Madeira	17 Aberdeen
9 Chelsea	18 Brussels

(Answers on page 153)

Useful recipes
from famous people 2

Here is **Spike Milligan's** contribution

Spaghetti à la Fred

Take a strand of spaghetti, lay it face downwards on a marble slab. Run a compass over the strand and find its magnetic north. Roll the strand in a solution of beaten egg yolk and Volnay '47. Take finely sliced garlic and pack carefully on each side of the spaghetti strand.

Take a copper pan, fill with water, and boil to 180° F or 201° C. Add a handful of salt. Drop strand into boiling water for fifteen minutes. When cooked to *à dente*, remove strand and serve with three fried eggs, mushrooms in wine sauce, chipolatas, steak, etc, etc.

Spaghetti song

(to be sung to the tune of *On Top of Old Smoky*)

On top of spaghetti,
All covered in cheese,
I lost my poor meatball,
When somebody sneezed.

It rolled off the table,
And onto the floor,
And then my poor meatball,
Rolled out of the door.

It rolled down the garden,
And under a bush,
And then my poor meatball,
Was nothing but mush.

A couple years later,
The bush was a tree,
So I can have meatballs,
To eat for my tea.

Spaghetti alla Casalinga

(serves about 40)

1 old hammock	margarine
1 Oxo cube	seasoning

Joint the hammock. Boil in a (galvanized) vat with the Oxo cube, taking care to set the soup aside after removing the spaghettini. Serve with a knob of margarine (keep it on a knitting-needle, and move rapidly from guest to guest, giving each a quick rub). *A tip*: save any leftovers; cold, and knotted together, they make wonderful hammocks.

(from *Punch*, 31 October 1973)

Useful recipes
from famous people 3

Here is **Mike Yarwood's** recipe for **Spaghetti Bolognese**

Mike Yarwood says 'this is one of my favourite recipes', and he sent it in specially for this book.

What you need
1 carrot, onion and stick of celery, chopped
200 gr (8 oz) of mince
1 small tin of tomatoes
1 dessertspoonful of tomato puree
beef stock
garlic, salt and pepper
500 gr (1 lb) of spaghetti
Parmesan cheese

How to make it
Gently fry the onion, carrot and celery until soft. Add the mince, tinned tomatoes, puree, seasonings, and enough stock to cover. Cook gently for half an hour. Cook the spaghetti in boiling water for about fifteen minutes. Drain. Pour sauce over the spaghetti and top with grated Parmesan cheese.

Please note The metric and imperial measurements given in recipes in this book are only approximately equivalent. So when you're measuring ingredients, stick to one or the other system.

Sam Stubbins's celebrated free food lecture 2
The secret of the rancid water-buffalo

Mrs Prendergast was one of the first to arrive for Sam's talk. As she walked up to her usual seat at the front of the hall, she saw something hanging down from the front of the platform. It was an enormous poster of strawberries. They were mouthwatering – huge, red, luscious and shining. Mrs Prendergast went nearer. She could have sworn she *smelt* them – a real, fruity, wafting smell of strawberries and summer.

And then – Whoosh! Goodbye, strawberries. From the side of the platform came an oniony, fried-steak-and-chips, sizzling-oil smell.

'Did you have to?' complained Mrs Prendergast, as Sam strode in. She'd been dreaming of white lace dresses, big hats, green lawns, delicate gold-rimmed teacups and summers long ago.

'I say,' said the Colonel, strolling up the hall and sniffing.

'Oh, good,' said Minty, following him. 'Is this going to be an Eat-in?'

Sam produced his hand from behind his back – with an aerosol can in it.

'Sorry, old mates,' he said. 'I can only afford the smell. Your actual food is too expensive. Now, there was a man, once, who owned a restaurant with all the latest gadgets – micro-wave ovens and frozen dinners. Didn't do very well. Trouble was, the customers missed the good old smell of food sizzling away in the oven, and bubbling in the saucepan. So he bought himself a can of this – cooking smells – and sprayed the place with it. Did very well after that.'

He handed the can down to Minty – it was labelled 'Cooking'.

'Now,' went on Sam, 'who likes butter?'

'Me,' said Mollie Pratt.

'Right, butter coming up. Try this can, Mollie.'

She sprayed the can around. Everyone jumped a mile.

'Ooh,' said Mollie, 'it's gone bad. It's all rancid. What a disgusting smell.'

Everyone looked rather pleased at that. Old Sam had been just a bit too clever this time. But the Colonel was nodding his head, and was about to speak when Sam broke in.

'It's all a matter of taste,' he said airily. 'Now once, when there was a famine in India, the Americans rushed off piles of butter there. Trouble was, the Indians didn't like it. Wouldn't touch the stuff. It didn't taste like the rancid water-buffalo butter they was used to. So . . . they rushed out cans of that stuff – your genuine taste of rancid water-buffalo butter – sprayed the American stuff, and everything was hunky-dory.'

'Who makes these things and *how*, might I ask?' said the Colonel.

'There's a firm called International Flavors and Fragrances. In New York. One of the biggest makers of smells in the world. What they do is, they analyse a real smell or taste, with a computer, to see what it's made of. It's all chemicals, anyway. Now, coffee – there's at least sixty different chemicals what make up that smell. Put them all together, and there you are. They've even made Coca-Cola, and that's supposed to be a deadly secret. Apple pie, mince pie, fresh orange juice, tomato soup, the smell of fresh paint, it's all the same to them. 'Course, strawberries, that's easy. They sell that to ice-cream makers, or the poster makers to put in the paper. Same with milk and chicken and beef. You put the beef-taste with your spun protein, and there you are – a beef burger.'

'Hmm,' said the Colonel. 'I don't think I like it. All this new-fangled messing about with food. It's not natural.'

''Course it's not,' said Sam. 'I quite agree. I mean, take all this stuff they put into white bread nowadays. Fat-extenders, and chlorine dioxide, and nitrogen peroxide, and sodium diacetate! Now in the old days they went about it naturally. When they wanted white flour, they dug up corpses and ground the bones to a fine powder – mixed it in – fee, fi, fo, fum. And of course, if sugar was expensive, then you'd naturally mix some sand in, to make up the weight. And suppose you was a sweetmaker, and you'd just finished painting the cart yellow, *and* you was making some yellow sweets just then – well, it's the most natural thing in the world to put some of the leftover paint into the sweets. That's economy. The bloke was fined for it, too, which seems a shame.'

'Well . . . I didn't mean . . .' blustered the Colonel.

'Went to a party the other night,' went on Sam regardless. 'Thought you might like a bite of the food . . .' and he began un-loading his pockets. It was a weird assortment of things, even for Sam. Everything was brilliantly coloured – orange, purple, red, green. He threw a deep purple round thing down to Bert, and said, 'Have a doughnut.'

Bert was still looking at it suspiciously when Sam held up a green thing. 'A sausage roll,' he said, and took a bite.

'Gives you quite a turn, doesn't it?' he added. 'But it's harmless, just vegetable dyes. And it's good to be suspicious. Makes you care-ful. But of course it's different when things *look* natural, and they aren't really. Like a brown kipper. Now, a kipper isn't brown, it's a dirty grey. So they dye it, 'cos it looks better like that. The only thing is, there's laws now, about what you can and can't do. Things are tested by experts. You've got to trust 'em, Colonel. Or grow your own stuff and cook it yourself. That could be your natural way, after all.'

Do you know?

Why holding your nose takes away nasty tastes?

Because there are only *four* tastes – sour, salty, sweet and bitter. You have tastebuds on your tongue which detect them. The ones on the tip of your tongue taste the sweet things, and the ones at the back taste the bitter things. All the other 'tastes' are really smells. The organ that detects *those* is in the back passages of your throat, which are linked to your nose. If you hold your nose, that interferes with the smelling, and you think you can't taste. (Same as with a bad cold.)

✳ A dog's sense of smell can be *a million times* more sensitive than a human's.

✳ Your tastebuds become less efficient as you get older.

✳ If you suck a lemon, sour things will taste much sweeter afterwards.

✳ There is a berry, which only grows in West Africa, which has the same effect, only much more powerfully. If you dissolve it on your tongue, sour things will taste quite sweet afterwards.

✳ If you wipe your tongue *dry* you won't be able to taste nearly so well.

How do you stop a fish smelling?
Cut off its nose.

Where does all the pepper go?
No one nose.

If all the world were paper,
    And all the seas were ink,
And all the trees were bread and cheese,
    What would we have to drink?

How to Avoid Tears when Peeling Onions

What are little boys made of?
   Frogs and snails,
    And puppy-dogs' tails;
And that's what little boys are made of.

What are little girls made of?
   Sugar and spice,
    And all that's nice;
And that's what little girls are made of.

What are young men made of?
   Sighs and leers,
    And crocodiles' tears;
And that's what young men are made of.

What are young women made of?
   Ribbons and laces,
    And sweet pretty faces;
And that's what young women are made of.

The lion and the unicorn were
   fighting for the crown;
The lion beat the unicorn all
   round about the town.
Some gave them white bread, some
   gave them brown;
Some gave them plum cake, and
   ran them out of town.

The cooking of art

Being the strange story of The Cheese-Race, and other items of food, past and present.

Cheese has been used as a food for over four thousand years. Using it as art is fairly new.

An artist called Dieter Rot had an exhibition in Los Angeles not so long ago, called The Cheese-Race. The exhibition consisted of forty suitcases, which he'd bought from all round Los Angeles – used suitcases, new suitcases, small ones, big ones – all filled with cheese. He found at least forty-eight different ways of putting cheese in suitcases. (Some of the suitcases had mirrors and all kinds of pockets and pouches in them.) He filled the suitcases with more than a ton of cheese. Then he meant to leave them in the exhibition for a month. He himself left after four days. By that time there was such a smell, he thought they would come and close down the exhibition.

Dieter Rot had had some Cheese-Races before. The way he did it, was to get lots of cheeses, mostly the soft kind, because they run better, and let them spread and ooze all over the place, racing each other. He'd put them on flat pieces of wood, stand the wood up – and they're off! (Lumps of hot chocolate made good racers, too.) But as Dieter Rot says, 'I have got a lot of experience with cheese, and I think hard cheeses don't give in so easily to a race, you know. They sit in the starting gate for years, sometimes. They don't move – then all of a sudden they go!'

And Dieter Rot isn't just a cheese artist. He has also made screen prints with chocolate, sculptures with meat, and for ten years he has got a great deal of satisfaction from pouring sour milk over his drawings.

(All this is fact, not fiction!)

If cheese comes after dinner,
what comes after cheese?
A mouse.

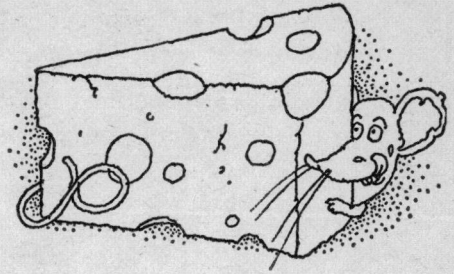

Penetrating the peculiar past of the potato

Potatoes originally came from way up in the Andes mountains in Peru. The Incas used to eat them – and make little clay pots shaped like potatoes with strange nobbles and faces on them. Then the Spaniards discovered them, about 1531, and brought them back to Europe.

There's a story that Sir Walter Raleigh first brought them to England. He *might* have brought some back to his estate in Ireland. Certainly, Sir Francis Drake got hold of some in 1578.

They had a funny start in England. Queen Elizabeth's Chamberlain invited all the nobles to dinner to try the new dish. Disaster. Everyone left with a stomach-ache, because the cooks had only used the leaves and stems (which are slightly poisonous) and left the potatoes themselves in the ground. That set back potato-cooking for some time.

People at first thought they caused leprosy and scrofula and rickets, and even TB. A sort of bad magic began to surround potatoes, so that even when people in Europe were starving, they wouldn't touch them. Frederick the Great sent a wagonload to a town called Kolberg, when food was very scarce. 'You must be joking,' said the people. 'They don't smell of anything – even the dogs won't eat them. What use are they?' Finally, he had to get an official to eat them publicly in the town square.

✱ If Sir Walter Raleigh brought back potatoes now, they would probably get banned. They contain a poisonous substance called solanine. There's only a tiny bit of it in good potatoes – not enough to hurt anyone. But if they turn green (that's when the sunlight has reached them) then they *are* dangerous, and you shouldn't eat them.

✱ The Irish eat a lot of potatoes. But the Paraguayans eat the most in the world – a quarter of a ton per person per year.

Useful recipes
from famous people 4

Here's **Tommy Steele's** favourite recipe for a winter's evening

Baked potato and cheese
'On a cold winter's evening, there's nothing I like better than a *large potato* baked in the oven (450° F, gas No 8) for about an hour. You then cut the potato in half, scoop some of the middle out, break an *egg* into it, and grate some *cheese* over it, with a little *butter*, and leave it under the grill for a few minutes.'

Why can't you ever starve in the desert?
Because of the sand which is there.

More venerable vegetables

An old Greek historian said that the labourers who built the Great Pyramid in Egypt lived on a diet of *onions, radishes* and *leeks*. Radishes used to be very large, so big that you had to cut slices off them, instead of popping the whole thing into your mouth at once. (French radishes are much bigger than ours, now.) As for leeks, they say that Nero, the Roman Emperor who fiddled while Rome burned, ate masses of them, to keep his voice in good trim.

The *cabbage* is another very old vegetable. The Romans said it was good for preventing drunkenness. You should eat some cabbage with vinegar before a big feast, and still more afterwards.

The redoubtable rabbit

Rabbits were first eaten in England about 1176. *Welsh Rabbits* have been eaten for a long time, too. Your genuine Welsh Rabbit is made with cheese, butter, a little brown ale, salt and pepper, all melted together in a saucepan, then poured, still bubbling, onto hot toast. You can make a very good dish rather like it, simply by grating some Cheddar cheese, mixing it with a bit of butter, mustard and

The Welsh Rarebit Machine

a spoonful of chutney. Then spread this paste onto toast, and grill it until it all melts into a gooey mass. The cheese cooks very quickly, so you have to watch it.

No one really knows where Welsh Rabbit got its name from. Some people say it was once a Welsh Rarebit, and the last name became shortened to Rabbit. Anyway, it doesn't hop, any more than a Bombay Duck quacks. Know what a Bombay Duck is? It's actually a fish, called a *bummalo*, which is dried and eaten with curry.

The most expensive banana in the world

Bananas were probably first grown in Asia. Alexander the Great saw them in India in 327 BC. But it wasn't until the end of the nineteenth century that they came to England. It's not hot enough to grow them here, so they're all imported, mostly from Central America. (So many bananas are grown there that countries like Honduras and Costa Rica got called Banana Republics.) And a banana goes bad if it's in a temperature cooler than 55° F. So it was only when refrigerators and refrigerated ships and trains got going that they could be sent abroad.

Lord Egremont told a story about his grandfather, Lord Leconfield, and a banana. When bananas were still a novelty in England, Lord Leconfield was eating one at dinner one night, with a friend. The friend said, 'Of course, this is nothing compared with a banana straight off the tree.'

So Lord Leconfield ordered his gardener to get a banana plant and grow him one. They built a greenhouse especially for the banana plant. They waited and waited. Finally, the plant bore fruit. One banana was brought before his Lordship on a grand dish. He cut a slice with a golden knife and put it in his mouth with a golden fork. Then he threw the whole lot away – knife, fork, dish and banana on the floor – and shouted:

'Oh God, it tastes just like any other damned banana!'

They say that banana cost him the best part of £3,000.

Useful recipes
from famous people 5

Here's a banana recipe from the first person to climb Mount Everest.

Sir Edmund Hillary's Banana Whip

What you need
3 large bananas, roughly mashed $\frac{1}{3}$ cup of sugar
1 white of egg, beaten stiffly   cream

How to make it
Fold the sugar into the egg-white. Then fold the bananas and serve instantly with cream. The dish must be made immediately before you mean to eat it. Serves two.

Where did they come from?

Cocoa
Cocoa was brought to Europe by the Spaniards from Mexico and Peru. It reached England in about 1652. They used to call it 'jocalette'.

Coffee
Coffee came to England at the end of the sixteenth century. The word 'coffee' comes from an Arabic word. Hundreds of coffee-houses opened in the seventeenth century – there were over five hundred of them in the City of London alone. They were great meeting places for people, like coffee-bars and snack-bars now.

Bread
The Egyptians were the first people to grind corn. Before that, it was roasted whole. So they were the first to make proper bread. They also discovered that leaving the dough made it rise better. They had acres and acres of corn stored in huge granaries, and from this they made over fifty different kinds of bread.

Sandwiches

Sandwiches were invented by the fourth Earl of Sandwich. He used to spend hours on end gambling at the gaming tables, and once, so that he wouldn't have to leave for a meal, he had some beef brought to him, in between two slices of bread. . . .

Wholemeal bread

What you need
1·5 kg (3 lbs) of wholemeal flour
3 teaspoonsful of salt
35 gr (1½ oz) of soft brown sugar
35 gr (1½ oz) of fresh yeast – or 2 level tablespoonsful of dried yeast
1 litre (1¾ pints) of warm water
large mixing bowl, small bowl, wooden spoon, loaf tins or cake tins

How to make it
The important thing about making bread with yeast is that everything must be *warm* – the bowl you mix it in and the water you use – so that the yeast grows and swells. A good place to leave the dough in is a really warm airing-cupboard.

1 Mix the yeast and sugar in the small bowl. Add 142 ml (¼ pint) of the *warm* water.

2 Leave this in a warm place for about 12 minutes, until it begins to froth. (That's the yeast beginning to work.)

3 Put the flour into the large *warm* mixing bowl. Sprinkle the salt round the edge, and make a well in the middle.

4 Stir the yeast mixture round, and then pour into the well of flour.

5 Add almost all the remaining warm water. (Keep a little bit out for the moment, until you see how dry the mixture is.)

6 Mix it all together with the wooden spoon at first, then with your hands, until you get a soft dough. If it's too dry, add the last of the water. Knead it until it feels springy.

7 Cover the bowl with a thick cloth or towel. Put in a *warm* place to rise for at least one hour.

37

8 Turn the dough out on to a floured board. Knead it well, pushing the dough away from you with the palm of your hand, then folding it backwards, then pushing it away again, and so on. Keep doing this for a while, until the dough is soft and springy.

9 Grease the two tins, and sprinkle some flour on them. Divide the dough into two, and put half into each tin. Take care that the dough does not touch the sides of the tins.

10 Put in a warm place again, for another half an hour.

11 The dough will rise again, almost doubling in size. Ten minutes or so before the half-hour is up, put the oven on to 425° F, gas No. 7.

12 Bake in the oven for one hour.

13 When the bread is cooked, the loaves will shrink away from the sides of the tin, and when you tap the bottom, it will sound hollow.

14 Turn the loaves out on to a cake-rack. Turn off the oven.

Sam Stubbins's celebrated free food lecture 3
Fabulous feasts

'I shall begin my lecture on fabulous feasts,' said Sam, 'with some booze.'

He then began to open a gigantic wine bottle on the table in front of him. There were about ten of them altogether.

' 'Ere, give us some,' came a voice from the back of the hall.

'Certainly,' said Sam. He ran from bottle to bottle, opening the tops and pouring them out helter-skelter.

Everyone began rushing to the front of the hall.

'What a waste!' cried Mrs Prendergast, beside herself. 'Quick, get some glasses, jugs, anything!'

There was wild dashing to and fro.

'It'll stain the floor,' shouted the caretaker. 'What the hell do you think you're doing?'

'It's all right,' shouted someone else. 'It's only white wine.'

But before anyone could catch it, the drink dripped away and disappeared through the floorboards.

Everyone sank back in their seats, exhausted.

'Just a little demonstration to get you in the mood,' said Sam, pleased with all the excitement. 'Only water, you know. Nothing to get het up about.'

There were sighs and oohs from the audience. Mrs Prendergast looked daggers.

'But old Henry V,' went on Sam, 'you know, the bloke who charged about at Agincourt and God for Harry and all that sort of thing – when *he* had his coronation feast, he did the thing properly. He had the whole palace yard running with claret and Rhine wine. 'Course, the Duke of Clarence, he was a geezer what did himself properly, too. Now, when *he* gave a banquet, he gave his guests little take-home presents. There they all were, sitting waiting for the pud, when – clickety-click – seventy horses came clattering right into the banqueting hall. And were they loaded? They were dripping with silver plate and cups and coats of armour and jewels and cloth of gold. Help yourselves, mates, says the Duke to all and sundry.'

'But what was the food like?' asked Mrs Prendergast.

'Not bad,' replied Sam, 'all things considering. Henry IV, now, he had a good old nosh-up for his marriage. In October 1399, that was. There was boar's head and tusks, cygnets (that's small swans, you know), pheasants, herons, sturgeon, pike, venison, stuffed sucking-pigs, peacocks, cranes, rabbits, bitterns, curlews, partridges, pigeons, quails and snipe. That was just the first course, naturally.'

'I say,' said Colonel Chumley-Mutt. 'Must have been a fine bit of shooting done in those days, what?'

'Disgraceful, I call it,' said Mollie Pratt. 'All them poor birds.'

'Which reminds me,' said Sam. 'If you're on top of a hill with a live swan in your arms, what's the quickest way to get down? Pluck the swan.'

There was a certain amount of groaning at that. Mrs Prendergast didn't get it.

'Actually, talking of shooting,' said Sam, 'it was once the food what was the ammunition. Now, King Charles, he was probably the finest shot with a roast chicken you could find. He had a do, back in 1667, on St George's Day, in the Banqueting Hall at Whitehall. Great big place. There he was, up on a throne, with all the Knights of the Garter at a whacking big table down the hall, and forty dishes of food for each Knight piled up high in front of them. Then Boom! off went the guns. Ta-ra! Ta-ra! that was the trumpeters trumpeting. And then they all started chucking food at each other. No kidding. Pepys wrote it all down in his Diary. Then in came a jester, cap and bells and all that, and jumped clean over everyone's heads, slap into a great bath of custard. That went down very well. 'Course, that's why knights wore armour, so they could have a quick sponge-down after a meal. Then there was puddings . . .'

Here, Sam whisked a tablecloth off something at the side of the stage. It was an enormous confection, bigger than three or four wedding-cakes. Made of sugar and marzipan, among other things, it was shaped like a castle with turrets and guns. There was a ship floating in the moat. There was a huge stag with an arrow sticking out of it. And all about were eggshells floating in the moat, and lots and lots of little pies.

Sam pulled the arrow out of the stag. Red wine ran down like blood. 'Let's have a bit of action,' he called, setting light to the guns. Boom! Gunpowder and smoke. 'Out you come,' he said, opening the pies. *Frogs* hopped out. *Live birds* came flying right out into the hall.

Mrs Prendergast leaped up in fright, which was a mistake, because she got hit on the nose by an eggshell. Sam was bombarding the hall with them.

'Not to worry,' he shouted, 'there's only rosewater in 'em. In the old days ladies used to like throwing 'em. Have a go, Mrs P.?'

But Mrs P. wasn't listening.

'Pity,' said Sam, sadly. 'It's all good clean fun, you know. All the best people used to do it.'

'Jolly good show, what?' said the Colonel. 'Reminds me of me young days – Hunt Balls, don't you know. Bread rolls whizzing, tarts . . .'

'Correction,' said Sam, helping a frog off the platform. 'All the best people *still* do it.'

They had a bit of trouble letting all the birds and frogs out of the hall, but eventually things quietened down.

Sam was bringing something out of his bottom right-hand pocket.

' 'Course, they *did* eat too much,' he said, pulling away at what looked like a long feather. It went on coming. About two feet of it. 'So a bloke called Walter Rumsey invented this. A stomach-brush. You put it down your throat like this . . .'

He had his mouth wide open and began shoving the thing down, but then, realizing he couldn't speak at the same time, and because he didn't really fancy doing it, he pulled it out again.

'Anyway,' he said, 'you put it right down into your stomach and stir it around. There's a little silk button on the end. Cleans the stomach. Then you start eating all over again. Yogis do it nowadays, you know. They put great long ropes down, and bring them up again.'

Sam had to stop there, because there was a gurgling noise coming from Mrs Prendergast. She seemed to be having a fit. Actually, she was quite all right when they helped her out of the hall, though she did say something about Sam Stubbins going too far, then stumped off home, muttering darkly.

The meeting broke up soon after that.

'I shall continue next week,' said Sam, 'with a further blood-curdling instalment of Breathtaking Banquets. Will those with a sensitive constitution please stay away.'

At this point the caretaker came rushing up.

'Here,' he said, 'what about all the mess, all those eggshells everywhere? Who's going to tidy it all up?'

'Oh dear,' said Sam. 'Up the workers. Me, I suppose.'

'I'm a worker, too,' said the Colonel. 'I'll give you a hand, old boy.'

'Me, too,' said Minty. 'If I can have what's left of the pudding.' Which she did.

Fabulous feast facts

✳ Ahasuerus, in the Old Testament, had a feast which went on for 160 days.

✳ In 1457, there was a banquet for the new Archbishop of York. They had: six wild bulls, 104 oxen, 1,000 sheep, 304 calves, 400 swans, 1,000 capons, 2,000 pigs, 104 peacocks, 13,000 other birds, 600 fish and a dozen porpoises and seals, among other things. With that there were 300 tuns of ale and 100 tuns of wine. (One tun = four hogsheads. One hogshead = 252 old wine-gallons.) How many people were there, I don't know.

✳ In the old days, kings and other important people were so afraid of being poisoned when they ate, that they often had special drinking cups. These were lined with rhinoceros horn, which was supposed to change colour if the drink was poisoned. Charles II, for one, kept his spoon and knife (he didn't use a fork) in his own locked box – so no one could tamper with them.

Do you know?

Why we drink toasts?

Before hops were used to flavour ale, people put toasted bread on the top, to flavour it. (Sometimes they used roasted crab-apples, too.) So the toast was actually part of the drink.

Food fit for a king

If you want to make something really special and delicious, try
Délicieuses de fromage
These are little balls of melted cheese, with a crisp outside. You can
eat them any time, with a fork or wooden stick.

What you need
200 gr (8 oz) of Cheddar – or any hard cheese that you can grate
    easily
2 egg-whites
fine breadcrumbs, toasted
a deep frying pan, oil for frying, a perforated spoon

How to make them
1 Grate the cheese.
2 Beat the egg-whites, just a little.
3 Mix the cheese and egg-whites together in a bowl. It's best to do it
with a spoon first, then your hands, until you have a solid ball, which
will be rather sticky.
4 Take a little bit of the mixture, and roll it into a ball in the palms
of your hands – no bigger than a marble.
5 Make all the mixture into little balls. Then roll them in the fine
dry breadcrumbs, to coat them.
6 Heat up enough oil in the pan to cover it to about 6 mm ($\frac{1}{4}''$).
Important Hot fat spits and can burn you. Treat it with great care
and get an adult to help you.
7 Put the cheese balls into the oil very gently, with a spoon. Try not
to let them stick together. Don't put in too many at once. You can
always do another lot afterwards.
8 Turn them over in the oil, until the whole outside of each ball is
light brown. This will only take a few seconds, so watch them very
carefully.
9 If you have more to cook, put the first lot on a plate. When they're
all cooked, hand them round immediately for eating. They stay hot
inside for quite a while.
10 Don't forget to turn the heat off, and move the frying pan off the
hotplate.

Royal fudge

Important note *Please* get an adult to help you with this. Hot sugar is dangerous. It burns, and it really hurts. Promise them half the fudge, if necessary!

What you need
1 kg (about 2 lbs) of granulated sugar
1 breakfast cup of milk
200 gr (8 oz) of butter
tin of Nestlé's condensed milk
1 teaspoonful of vinegar
chopped nuts (or raisins)
a large heavy saucepan that food won't stick to (very important)
a wooden spoon to stir with
a baking tin to put the fudge in to set

How to make it
This will make a lot – but it will keep for quite a long time in a tin (if you *can* keep it). If you haven't got a very large saucepan, then use half the amounts.

1 Put the sugar and half the butter and the cup of milk into the heavy saucepan.
2 Stir all this over a gentle heat, until the sugar melts.
3 Turn the heat up a little, and let the mixture bubble. *Keep watching it*. If it bubbles up too high and looks as if it will boil over, take it off the heat for a while, or turn the heat down. Let it boil gently until it turns a golden brown. This then means that the sugar has caramelized (takes about 10 minutes).
4 Add the Nestlé's milk.
5 Boil gently again for about 10 minutes.
6 Take the saucepan off the heat and turn the hotplate off. Add the rest of the butter, which should be cut up into small pieces, and the vinegar. Stir until the butter is quite melted. Now add nuts, or raisins, as you like. (It's good plain, though; and a few drops of vanilla essence make it taste even better.)
7 Grease the baking tin. Pour the mixture in.
8 Wait for about half an hour, until the mixture sets a bit. Cut into squares.

This is very easy to make, and it's a delicious crunchy fudge. The only trouble you might get is if the sugar begins to burn the bottom of the saucepan – you'd then see dark brown streaks appearing in the mixture. If this happens, turn the mixture into another saucepan, and go on from there. If it still burns and goes streaky, pour it into the baking tin all the same, before it burns too much. It often tastes pretty good like this, even though it might not look so marvellous!

Food for special occasions

Christmas food

Boar's head used to be the treat for Christmas, not turkey. (They say the heroes in Valhalla feasted continually on boar's flesh.) Then in

the old days there used to be *peacocks* and *capons, swans* and *pheasants* and *geese*.

Turkeys came to Europe from America. William Strickland brought them in the sixteenth century. And we got the idea of eating them for a special-occasion meal from the Americans, too. Over there, Thanksgiving Day in November is traditionally celebrated with a grand turkey meal. But, even a hundred years ago in England, you would have been most likely to get a goose for Christmas dinner (if you were lucky) rather than turkey.

Christmas pudding dates from about 1670. Before then, it wasn't a solid pudding, but more like a soup. It was called 'plum-porridge' – made of meat-broth and plums.

Mince-pies started life as 'minced pies', made with meat – 'neats' tongues, chicken, eggs, sugar, raisins, lemon and orange peel and various kinds of spicery'. (Neats' tongues were ox-tongues.)

Easter food

Hot-cross buns were first made in about AD 600. Before then, the Anglo-Saxons used to eat a special bun in honour of their goddess, Eastre. Then, when Christianity came, and the feast of Eastre became Easter, the clergymen thought they had better get rid of all this pagan nonsense, so they put a cross on the buns, to make them Christian, too.

Easter eggs Eggs have been eaten, especially in the spring-time, since pre-Christian times. Greeks, Romans, Egyptians and Persians were among those who thought of the egg – which is the beginning of life – as the symbol of spring. Our Easter eggs are part of that tradition.

Also, in England, eggs used to be forbidden during Lent. So one way of keeping them was by hard-boiling them. And then when Lent was over, there were masses of eggs waiting to be eaten, because the hens didn't know they ought to stop laying.

If you hard-boil your own eggs, you can decorate them for Easter by drawing straight on to them with wax crayons, and then scratching a pattern in the wax. Or you could just paint a picture on them with a paintbrush, or draw with felt-tip pens. Or you can dye eggs while you're boiling them – onion-skin in the boiling water will

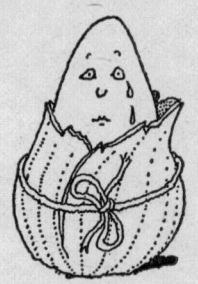

turn them a browny colour. Saffron will make them yellow, and cochineal gives a good red. If you tie the onion-skins on to an egg itself, then you get an interesting pattern. If the eggs crack, though, and air gets in, then they go bad and stink. To make them last, the best thing is to blow the inside out of a raw egg, in the following way.

With a large darning needle, make a hole in both ends of the egg. Be very careful – the egg-shell is hard, and easy to crack. Widen the holes a little. (If a bit cracks away from the hole, it doesn't matter – it will make it easier to blow.) Then hold the egg over a bowl, with the large end uppermost. Put the needle through to the middle of the egg several times, to make sure that the yolk is broken. Then blow gently but steadily. It's hard at first, but gradually the white, and then the yolk, will run through. Then you can paint or draw on the egg. If you thread cotton through, and tie a little button at one end, then the egg can be hung up.

✳ The largest-ever chocolate egg was made for a South African visitor to London. It was ten feet high and contained nearly half a ton of sweets and chocolates. Then there was another kind of Easter egg, a real monster. It was so big that it had to be delivered outside the house, and left on the lawn. Then part of it slid to one side, and out trotted two ponies, pulling a carriage. There was an attendant riding on top, too.

✳ Up in the north of England they play 'jarping' with hard-boiled eggs. You hit each other's eggs, like playing conkers, and the person whose egg breaks first has to eat it.

Haggis
A haggis looks rather like a soft hand-grenade. It's a special Scottish

dish, traditionally eaten on Burns Night (15 January), St Andrew's Day (30 November), Martinmas (11 November) and Hogmanay (31 December). The Romans first made it, out of pig mince, raw eggs, pineapple and liquamen, which is a kind of Roman Worcester sauce made of fish and spices and wine. They called it *hagas*. But the Ancient Scots hated pigs, so they made it with mutton, the hearts, lungs and liver of sheep, oatmeal, suet, onions, pepper, salt and herbs. All that is wrapped up in the stomach-bag of a sheep. 'Haggis Royal' is served with venison sauce.

✳ There's a big export market for tinned haggis!

✳ There's a shortage of haggis-stitchers – who sew the sheep's stomach-bag neatly round all the ingredients.

Food quiz 2
Guess what?

A house painted red outside, white inside, and black people live in it.

An apple.

Me riddle, me riddle.
A wee, wee man,
With a red, red coat,
A stick in his hand,
And a stone in his throat.
If you read me this riddle,
I'll give you a groat.

A cherry

In marble walls as white as milk,
Lined with a skin as soft as silk;
Within a fountain crystal clear,
A golden apple does appear.
No doors are there to this stronghold,
Yet thieves break in and steal the gold.

An egg

Once a year, a businessman retires to a monastery for a week's peace and quiet. He's been doing this for ages, and every year he asks for an orange, an apple and a piece of string.

One year, the Abbot, dying of curiosity, asked him why he wanted these three things. The businessman told him, but swore him to secrecy. And the Abbot, being a man of God, kept his word . . .

Sam Stubbins's celebrated free food lecture 4

Given in the village hall of Little Nibbling, by kind permission of the caretaker – on condition that Sam clears up the mess himself afterwards.

Breathtaking banquets

'Now take Lord Mayors' banquets,' said Sam. 'They was real beanos. You know what a beano is?'

'It's a comic,' said Steve.

'That's right,' said Sam. 'A feast of old jokes what you swallow down in one go. Well, the old Greeks actually had a *beanfeast*. It was in honour of their god Apollo, who was the God of Beans. Full of beans, the old Greeks were. And this great beanfeast got so talked about that it got to be the name for any big feast, and then it got shortened to a beano, then it got turned into a comic . . . where was I?'

'Lord Mayors' beanos,' called a voice.

'Ah yes. They still have 'em, you know, but not so grand. This year, do you know what the menu was?'

Sam drew from his pocket a very grand, gold and red menu, emblazoned with coats of arms and golden tassels, and began to read from it. 'Fish soup, sole, roast partridge with spuds and green beans, then nut pudding and black cherries. That's all. No choice, either. 'Course, they did have five wines, and the Honourable Artillery Company playing music. But stands to reason, they've got to leave

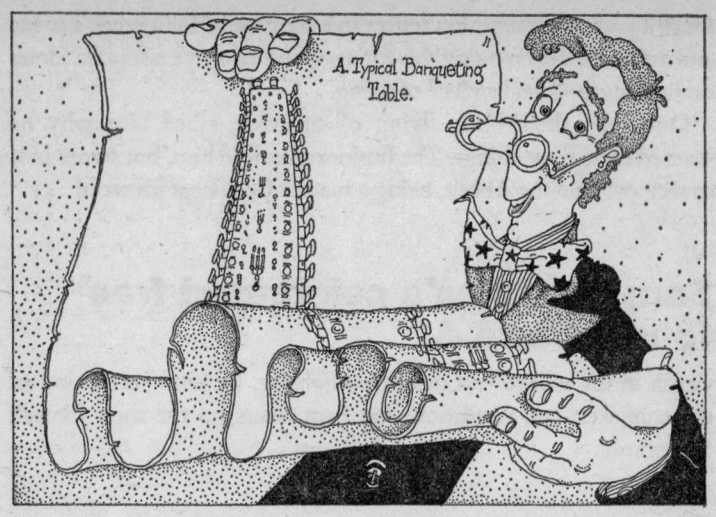

A Typical Banqueting Table.

room for all the speeches they've got to stomach afterwards ...
Now, back in 1828, they started with two hundred tureens of turtle
soup. Made from real turtles. That was the most expensive soup
ever, and a sort of greenish colour. And just *one* of the puddings was
two hundred dishes of different ice-creams!'

'What about the workers?' called someone.

'What a shocking waste,' cried Mollie Pratt.

Mrs Prendergast said nothing – because she wasn't there, not this
time.

'The workers was working, same as usual,' said Sam, 'and lucky
to get a sniff at a piece of meat. But Queen Victoria, when she was
crowned, she gave a meal for two thousand charity children in
Brighton. They had half a pound of roast beef each, plum pudding
and a glass of wine. Meat was getting a bit scarce even then, you
know. That's why some geezer in Paris got sold on the idea of horsemeat. Gave a horsemeat banquet, so as the idea would catch on.
There was horse soup and then boiled horsemeat and cabbage. Don't
know what the horse-pudding was like.'

'Did it catch on, then?' asked Bert.

'What do you think?' said Sam. 'I reckon those days are over, though. The last really big banquet I know of was in Paris, in 1905. That was for forty thousand people.'

'Aren't there any nowadays?' asked Minty. 'I like to hear about them.'

'There was one, not so long ago. Given by the Shah of Iran. His family had been on the Peacock Throne for two and a half thousand years, so he celebrated, for a week. All the schoolchildren had the week off school, by the way. It wasn't so big, though, only six hundred people. But they was the real bigwigs – kings and heads of state. The Duke of Edinburgh went, and so did Princess Anne. There was music in a minstrels' gallery, and great crystal chandeliers and goldplated cutlery. They brought cooks from Maxim's in Paris, and from St Moritz and Monte Carlo, all the best places. I'll tell you what they ate: quails' eggs stuffed with golden Imperial caviar; mousse of crayfish tails; roast saddle of lamb with truffles; sorbet of Moët et Chandon (that's champagne ice); fifty peacocks with their feathers, surrounded by roast quails and served with nut and truffle salad; fresh figs and cream; raspberries and port wine; and coffee and cognac Prince Eugène.

' 'Course, there was a different wine with each course. Funny thing was, seeing as how it was his own banquet, the Shah didn't like caviar, so he had artichoke hearts instead. Maybe it was that "golden Imperial" bit – thought it might have been a bit hard on the Imperial teeth.'

'What are truffles?' asked Mollie.

'Kind of mushroom,' replied Sam, 'grows underground. They use pigs to go and sniff them out.'

'And what are quails?' asked Minty.

'Little birds,' said Sam. 'You can buy them over here. People have special quail farms. It's enough to turn you vegetarian, all the bird-eating that goes on. They do say that peacocks are terrible tough things. Maybe everyone was too polite to say so.'

✳ The menu for Princess Anne's wedding breakfast was:
oeufs Drumkilbo – scrambled egg with lobster, shrimps and tomato, bound in mayonnaise
perdreau en cocotte bonne femme – partridge with mushrooms, onion and bacon rolls, served with peas, cauliflower, new potatoes and salad
bombe glacée royale – peppermint ice-cream, filled with grated chocolate and eaten with biscuits

Guess what?
A hard day's night

This 'poem' looks like double Dutch. But it isn't. It's got rhyming slang in it – mostly Cockney, from the East End of London. For instance, instead of saying 'wife', you say 'carving-knife', which rhymes with it. And, 'See you alligator', instead of 'See you later'. If you can't translate this, the right words are given on page 153.

Bill Bloggs came home
One night and saw
His carving-knife
Was at the door.

She gave him a butcher's
From her mince-pies,
And said, 'Bill Bloggs,
Don't tell me lies,
Or try to be funny,
Where's the bees and honey?
You're elephant's trunk,
I'm telling you.'

'Too Irish stew,'
Poor Bloggsey said,
'Oh, me loaf of bread.
Now, just you cut
The rabbit and pork,'
And he tried to walk
Up the apples and pears.

But his bacon and eggs
Fell out with his plates,
Like they'd never been mates,
And his quaker oat
Had a fight with his throat,
And his this and that
Got flung on the mat,
And his Dicky dirt
Got grievously hurt ...

'Here, me old pot and pan,'
Said his wife, and ran,
And shoving him plumb
In the fife and drum,
She stripped him stark
In the Noah's ark,
And said, 'Bill Bloggs,
Now just you mark,
It's like I said,
I keeps yer round the houses,
And *you* keeps yer Uncle Ned.'

Greedy guts

There was an old fellow of Duns,
Who swore he'd eat ninety-nine buns.
   At the seventy-first,
   He unhappily burst,
And the rest were consumed by his sons.

At six o'clock one evening, someone saw Louis XIV eat: four full
plates of different soups; a whole pheasant; a partridge; a large
plateful of salad; two big slices of beef; some mutton in gravy; a
plateful of tarts and cakes; some fruit and some hard-boiled eggs.

   Then at ten o'clock he felt rather hungry, so he had a good supper.

Louis XV had for supper one day: currants; egg soup with
lemon juice (twenty spoonsful); broth; eight cockscombs; some
boiled chicken; boiled veal; the marrow of a bone; a wing and a half
of chicken roasted and fried in breadcrumbs; jelly; a sugar horn
filled with apricots; sugared chestnut; preserved cherries; a little
bread, and some fennel biscuits.

   He was ten years old at the time.

And they say a Roman called Clodius Albinus, who was over here
on government business, could manage to eat in one morning: five
hundred figs; one hundred peaches; ten melons; twenty pounds of
grapes; ten figpeckers (little birds); and four hundred oysters.

How much government business he managed to do after all that is not recorded.

A boy called Matthew Daking, aged twelve, ate 136·57 kg (384 lbs 2 oz) of food in six days – but he was suffering from a disease called *bulimia*, which means you just have to eat and can't stop.

Crazy cookery
How to make pebble soup

One day, a ragged young man knocked on the door of a farmhouse.

'Can you spare a bit of food?' he asked the farmer's wife. 'I'm very hungry.'

'No, I can*not*,' said the woman firmly. 'There's nothing in the house at all.' And she slammed the door.

The young man knew there must be *something* to eat. But how was he to get at it? He thought for a while, then he opened the door a crack, and called through, 'Are you interested in cooking? Have you ever made pebble soup?'

The woman *was* interested. Pebble soup! What an economical idea. So she asked the young man into her kitchen, to show her how to make it. He scooped up a handful of stones from outside, and came in. First, he carefully washed the stones. Then he put them in a large saucepan, and filled it with water, then added salt, and stirred it all over the fire.

'It'll take a bit of time to cook,' he said, so the woman got on with her work.

After a while, he tasted a bit in a spoon. 'Mmm, delicious,' he said. 'It's going to be good. But it's a pity you haven't got a carrot. It would make all the difference.'

'Oh well,' said the woman. 'I have got a couple somewhere.' (She didn't want to spoil the soup.)

The young man stirred the pebbles and carrots, and tasted again.

'Yes,' he said. 'That's excellent. Of course, an onion is really part of the recipe, but you haven't got one, so we'll have to do without.'

Well – the woman *did* have an onion. She gave it to the young man.

The water bubbled. The pebbles, carrots and onion simmered gently. The young man tasted again. 'That's it,' he said. 'I think we've got it now. Almost. But there is one thing that makes all the difference between really good and The Very Best pebble soup, and that's a beef-bone . . .'

He shook his head sadly. Now, by this time, the woman was desperately keen to try the soup. She toddled off to the larder again, and produced a beef-bone.

'That's marvellous,' said the young man. 'I'll leave it just a little while longer, because the pebbles aren't quite done yet.' And he industriously stirred the soup.

At last it was ready. The woman laid the table with bowls and a hunk of brown bread each. The young man very carefully ladled out the soup from the top of the saucepan, and filled the bowls. The soup was delicious – delicately flavoured with onions and carrots and a good beef-bone.

'What do you think?' he asked.

'You're quite right,' said the woman. 'It's very good. Fancy that. Pebble soup.'

When they'd finished, the young man said goodbye. She waved to him from the farmhouse door as he disappeared quickly down the road. She then went back to the stove, and looked in the saucepan to see if there was any soup left. And there at the bottom, just exactly the same as when they were first put in, she saw the pebbles, hard and stony. But by that time, the young man, well-fed and happy, was far, far away ...

The brilliant invention of Doctor Who?

Cornflakes were invented in Battle Creek, Michigan, USA, at the end of the nineteenth century. By whom? And why?

Listen ... all over the Middle West of America mouths are opening, knives and forks are scraping, teeth are chewing – fried hunks of pork, great lumpy masses of corn are gurgling down into the American stomach. Listen again ... the American stomach is complaining, growling, moaning, grumbling, rumbling – until at last, Burp! Belch! Pardon! The American stomach strikes again.

The better-off people *dined* on fried steak, *lunched* on fried steak, *breakfasted* on fried steak. American inns advertised: 'Eat all you want. Twenty-five cents. Whisky, five cents extra.' Then start your morning with two kinds of meat, plus bread and potatoes, salt, pepper and pickles, eggs, toast and hot cakes, biscuits and butter. Have some cheese to round it off. Then go and sit behind a desk. It'll soon be time for lunch ...

Stop, Stop, STOP! Enough is enough, and as good as a feast. You can't go on like this. Unfair to stomachs. Lots of people began saying that. One of them was a Dr Kellogg. He was a Seventh-Day Adventist, an inventor, a doctor, a vegetarian, a believer in Pure and Healthy Food. And he lived in Battle Creek, Michigan, and ran the Battle Creek Sanatorium. It was a cross between a grand hotel, a health farm and a hospital. The kind of place James Bond has to go to, in the course of duty.

And there, in the kitchens, Dr Kellogg racked his brains over breakfast. What could he make that was pure, and light on the stomach? Something toasted and wafer-thin and pre-digested?

And then he got wind of epoch-making news. Up in Niagara Falls, a Mr Perky was said to be stretching out wheat grains and squeezing them through little holes and making little mattresses called Shredded Wheat.

The Doctor swore: 'I can do it, too – and better.' So he and Mrs Kellogg and his brother W. K., and some of his forty adopted children, got to work. They soaked and boiled wheat grains. Mrs Kellogg rolled them out on the pastry board. It all stuck together in one great gluey mess. And then the Doctor had a dream. He saw how to do it. He let the wheat stand for some time, and *then* he rolled it out. Each little wheat grain turned into a single flake, which they scraped off and baked in the oven.

That was a start. They got bigger rollers, bigger ovens. But then the stuff went mouldy, so they removed the wheat germ and used the rest. The rollers got too hot, so they filled them with water. The heat wasn't right for the toasting, so they put it right. And then they started using corn instead of wheat. And so the Cornflake was born.

Then the rush started. Down in Battle Creek, the word swept around. 'Dr Kellogg can make something out of ordinary corn that sells for ten times as much.'

Corn into gold! So the Gold Corn Rush started. Suddenly the town began to hum and rattle as the rollers rolled and the ovens baked. Every house, every shed, became a cornflake factory. People came from everywhere, and if there wasn't a house to spare, then they put up tents, till Battle Creek looked like Indian Territory – the cornflake makers had come to town. And the boiling and the baking and the steaming filled the air.

In Battle Creek, in the early 1900s, you could choose your breakfast from Grape Nuts, Grip Nuts, Postum Cereal, Hullo Boena, Hello-Billo, Cero-Fruto, Shredded Wheat, Fruito-Cerro, Malt-Ho, Flake-Ho, Abita, Tryachewa, Corn Crisp, Korn Kure, Korn Pone, Oatsina, Hayina, Strawina . . .

And then the companies that had blossomed overnight folded, fell away, like flowers in a thunderstorm. Not Kellogg's, though. They prospered. The Doctor got fed up with business, and sold out to his brother, W. K. Kellogg. W. K. spent millions on advertising.

He ran his competitors out of business. He made sure that his product tasted better and fresher than any of the others. And he made sure that his initials, W.K., were on every packet of cornflakes. The Doctor was furious. (He always hated his brother, and they fought all their lives!) And for fifty years the initials stayed. Not any more, though. Now it's just Kellogg's, so maybe the Doctor won in the end.

There's a twist to this story. Dr Kellogg invented cornflakes as a Health Food. But in order to make his Fresh, Pure flakes, he took the germ out of the corn; and in that germ were B vitamins, and they were good. He didn't know it but he'd removed the most nourishing part of his food, for corn is mostly carbohydrate. So when this fact became known, the cornflake people put back the B vitamins they took out. You can see them listed on the side of every packet.

As for Dr Kellogg himself – he was a superman. He kept going, inventing, being a surgeon, mesmerizing the rich into giving up drink and meat. He invented peanut butter. He travelled the world in pursuit of good diets and new medicine. In 1943, at the age of ninety-one, he ran up and down a cinder track most of the day in Battle Creek, for the benefit of press photographers. They gave in before he did. He was still dressed, as always, in white from top to toe – white hat, white spectacles, white suit, white shoes. He died the next year, I'm sorry to say. But his name hasn't.

More brilliant inventions
Coca-Cola

Coca-Cola was invented by a man called John S. Pemberton, who originally sold it as a *brain tonic* and general pick-me-up. There's a bit of truth in this. Coke has some caffeine in it, and caffeine is a drug. (It's also in coffee and tea.) A bottle of Coke has as much caffeine as a third of a cup of coffee. The caffeine in Coca-Cola comes from cola seeds.

The 'coca' part of the name comes from the belief that Coca-Cola essence used to be made from coca leaves. Coca is a Peruvian shrub from which is extracted cocaine, a powerful drug. Maybe it was used in 1886, when Coke was first made, but Coca-Cola certainly doesn't contain any now!

What exactly *is* it now? It is 99% sugar and water and carbon dioxide, to make it fizzy. The other 1% is a mixture (known only to two men, they say), of caramel colouring, flavouring and caffeine. This essence, this 1%, is sent all over the world. Then the sugar, water and fizz are added, put into the special bottles, lots of money is spent on advertising – and the whole world has a Coke. They call it Coca-Colanization.

✳ Tierra del Fuego, right down at the bottom tip of South America, is one of the few places in the world where you *can't* buy Coca-Cola. (They don't have white flour or sugar, either.)

Fish fingers

Fish fingers were invented by an American called Mr Birdseye. He called them Fish Sticks. 'Fish fingers' is the English name for them. Up in Grimsby, they freeze more than anywhere else in the world.

At the time I'm writing, they're usually made of cod. The fish is sliced and flattened and frozen into slabs. Diamond saws rotate at seven thousand revs per minute to slice the slabs into fingers. Then the fingers move along a conveyor belt and get showered with flour-and-water batter, then smothered in yellow breadcrumbs. Then they go through a frier for one minute to seal the batter – then off the end of the belt, into the packet, into lorries, into shops, and into you.

But – cod is getting scarce and expensive. So now they have to look for other fish never caught and used before. Down in the depths of the sea, five hundred fathoms down where the water is dark, there lurk great, strange, bulgy-eyed fish. There's the rat-tail fish, otherwise called the *grenadier* – and the *black scabbard* and *geph yoberi darwinii*. Maybe, by the time you read this, they won't be whole fish any more, they'll be fish fingers.

✳ More than one thousand million fish fingers are eaten in Britain every year.

Ice-cream

There are two kinds of ice-cream you can buy – Dairy Ice-cream, which must have some *whole milk* in it, and Ice-cream, which doesn't. The 'cream' part of the latter is a little bit of skim milk (the milk that's left *after* you've removed the cream!) and vegetable oils.

All the same, this ice-cream does *look* creamy, so how do they do it? Lyons Maid Raspberry Ripple is made up of: 62·2% water; 25·4% sugar of various kinds; 8·3% vegetable fats; 2·9% protein from 8% skim milk powder – and the streaks of 'raspberry' are pink-coloured and artificially flavoured. The 'ice-cream' has emulsifiers and stabilizers in it, to make it stay smooth and cream-like. Then the whole lot is whipped up with the same amount of *air* to make it light and fluffy.

✴ Someone once ate 3·3 kg (7 lbs 3 oz) of ice-cream in half an hour.

Baked beans

Heinz have been making baked beans since the beginning of this century. They get little white beans, from France and other countries. Then they get especially red tomatoes, grown for them in Portugal and Turkey. The tomatoes are mushed up and mixed with spice and cornflour. Then salt-water and sugar syrup are pumped in.

Meanwhile, the beans are sorted, washed, blown dry, sized and thrown into a huge trough of hot water. Then they go through infra-red ovens for a few seconds to bake them. That's the beans done. The cans are half-filled with them, and topped up with the sauce. Then the tins are cooked in huge sterilizers, to make sure the baked beans don't go bad. Finally, whirr, whirr, along the conveyor belt and out the other end.

✴ A boy called Melvin Roberts, of Ashby-de-la-Launde in Lincs, is reputed to live on nothing but baked beans on toast, twice a day. There is quite a lot of protein in them, and vitamin C in the tomatoes – but they are *not* the perfect complete meal.

✴ Heinz sell 1,250,000 tins of baked beans per *day*.

✴ Baked beans have been eaten for centuries, long before Mr Heinz was thought of. The French, for instance, have a delicious dish called

cassoulet, which is made of haricot beans baked slowly in the oven with pork, onions, herbs, garlic and goose or lamb. And *Boston Baked Beans* is a famous old American dish. It's a mixture of beans, baked in a big pot for hours, with onion, brown sugar, mustard, and molasses (treacle).

Sausages

In the UK there's a law about sausages. Pork sausages must be at least 65% meat. Beef sausages only have to be 50% meat. The rest is mostly wetted bread, with salt and spices and herbs to make them tasty. They also contain chemical preservatives. They are wrapped in skins traditionally made from animal intestines, though a lot of skins now are artificial. Pork sausages can have other meat in them, besides pork.

The *frankfurter* started life in Germany, before it went to America and became a hot dog. It's made of pork which is lightly smoked. *Salami* is made in one long roll, with lumps of white fat in it. You don't have to cook this; you just cut a slice and eat it. Most Continental sausages are made with smoked or salted meat, so that they keep for a long time.

Margarine

Margarine was invented in 1869 by a chemist's assistant called Hippolyte Mège Mouriès. (They say that Napoleon III was desperate for a butter substitute to feed his soldiers on, and that's why people were on the lookout for it.) Mouriès made it out of animal fat, called beef tallow. The Dutch developed the idea. They exported their butter, and ate margarine at home. They made margarine out of vegetable oils, which were cheaper. Coconut oil can be used as well, and palm kernel oils. (In Germany in 1911, they used whale oil.)

The crude oil is transported in huge tankers. The oil is pumped into enormous vats and treated with caustic soda. What goes to the bottom is made into soap, and the rest is made into margarine.

(That's why Unilever, who make Stork margarine, also make soap – killing two birds with one drop of oil. And in the Second World War, margarine *and* soap were rationed by the Ministry of Food.)

The oil is then bleached – to remove the smell – and it's heated at 180° C for six hours; then hydrogen is added, then emulsifier to make it smooth and solid, then colouring, flavour and vitamins (A and D).

✳ Stork have spent about £250,000 getting the taste right. They add twenty separate flavours which are found in butter.

Tomato ketchup

Ketchup (or catchup or catsup) comes from a Chinese word, *ke-tsiap*, which means the juice that fish are pickled in. You can have mushroom ketchup and walnut ketchup as well as tomato.

Tomato ketchup is made from tomatoes, sugar, vinegar, salt and spices. The Spaniards started it. They found tomatoes growing wild – little ones – in Peru and Mexico, and brought them back to Spain. They were used for decoration first. Then a Spanish Court Chef began mixing them with oil, vinegar, onions and pepper.

A mixed bag of food jokes

Have you heard about the Scotsman who went into a restaurant? He managed to sneak out without eating . . .

'Waiter, why have you got your thumb on my steak?'
'Well, I don't want to drop it on the floor again, do I?'

A hungry old goat called Heather,
Was tied up with an old piece of leather.
　In a minute or two,
　She chewed it right through,
And that was the end of her tether.

A friend of Bill Hawkins knocked on his door one day. 'Where's Bill?' he asked his wife.

'He's just died,' replied the woman. 'He went down the garden to cut a cabbage for lunch, tripped over the wheelbarrow, knocked his head on the shed door, fell over the motor-mower, and the garden fork went clean through his heart.'

'Good heavens! What did you do?'

'Only thing I *could* do. Opened a tin of peas.'

And have you heard of the wife who put her newly cremated husband's ashes into an egg-timer? Well, the lazy good-for-nothing had never done any work in his life . . .

A glutton, who came from the Rhine,
Was asked at what hour he would dine.
 He said, 'At eleven,
 At ten, five and seven,
And eight, and a quarter to nine.'

Crazy cookery
To make an Amblongus Pie, by Edward Lear

Take four pounds (say four and a half pounds) of fresh Amblongusses, and put them in a small pipkin.

Cover them with water and boil them for eight hours incessantly, after which add two pints of new milk, and proceed to boil for four hours more.

When you have ascertained that the Amblongusses are quite soft, take them out and place them in a wide pan, taking care to shake them well previously.

Grate some nutmeg over the surface, and cover them carefully with powdered gingerbread, curry powder and a sufficient quantity of Cayenne pepper.

Remove the pan into the next room, and place it on the floor. Bring it back again, and let it simmer for three-quarters of an hour.

Shake the pan violently till all the Amblongusses have become of a pale purple colour.

Then, having prepared the paste, insert the whole carefully, adding at the same time a small pigeon, two slices of beef, four cauliflowers, and any number of oysters.

Watch patiently till the crust begins to rise, and add a pinch of salt from time to time.

Serve up in a clean dish, and throw the whole out of window as fast as possible.

Sam Stubbins's celebrated free food lecture 5
The secret of the black plimsolls and the white rabbit

Sam Stubbins strode on to the platform, and gave a small bow to the audience. There was some clapping – and some jeers from the back of the hall.

'Thank you,' said Sam. 'Today, I am going to talk about clothes.'

'What about food?' came a voice from the back.

Sam took no notice. 'Boots and shoes first,' he said. 'Can some kind gentleman lend me his footwear, please?'

There was silence.

'Come on, Bert,' said Sam. 'Lend us your boots.'

Bert Jenkins bent down and took off his boots, shaking his head.

'Pass them forward, there's a good chap,' said Sam, and he leant over the platform. Several people held their noses, but eventually the boots reached his outstretched hands. He put them on the table, beside his glass of water.

'I *may*,' declared Sam, 'eat these boots.'

(Cries of 'Garn', 'Let's see you, then' and 'Get on with it'.)

'But that depends on you,' continued Sam. 'And that reminds me of a story, a very sad story about the Eskimo missionary. He happened to be on an ice floe, way up in the frozen north. Driftin', you understand. All on his tod. Well, he was desperate, 'cos he hadn't any food and he didn't fancy drinking sea water – thought it might send him ravin' bonkers. At last, he decided to eat his boots. He managed to get them undone, and he was just going to start chewing them, when he sneezed. It was a mighty big sneeze. A real whopper. And he sneezed his false teeth right into the ocean, where they sank down into fathoms of icy water. Now, those boots might've been food. And these boots' – pointing to Bert's battered specimens – '*are* food, if you're desperate. And I,' went on Sam, dramatically, 'will publicly eat these revolting looking things, *if* ' – ignoring Bert's ''Ere, steady on' – 'any one of you can tell me what food really is.'

There was immediate uproar in the hall. Shouts from all over.

'Fish and chips.'

'Bread.'

'Cabbage.'

'Bangers and mash.'

'Ice-cream.'

'Doughnuts' – from Bert.

'Frogs and snails and puppy-dogs' tails,' yelled the jokers at the back.

'And what are they?' said Sam, very pleased with himself.

There was silence.

'Food,' shouted someone.

Everyone realized they were going round in circles. Baffled silence again.

'Food,' said Sam impressively. 'Any kind of food that comes from *any* living animal or plant is basically **carbon**, with nitrogen, hydrogen, oxygen and some sulphur and other minerals.'

'You mean just a lot of nasty chemicals?' called Mrs Prendergast.

'That's right,' said Sam. He took something out of a deep pocket in his large overcoat. It was a black lump of something.

'Now,' went on Sam, 'here's some charcoal. That's almost pure carbon. What do you think of that, Mrs Prendergast? Is it food? Shall I eat it?'

'Yes, go on, smartie, stuff it down.' The back of the hall was getting impatient.

'Well . . . I don't know,' said Mrs Prendergast. 'You said it was. But I wouldn't fancy it myself.'

But Sam was getting something out of *another* pocket – a ball of wool. He chucked it to the back of the hall. 'There you are, my friend,' he said to the unruly element, 'help yourself. There's a sweater for you.'

Then he continued with his talk. 'Now, this charcoal's like that ball of wool. Charcoal ain't food. Your stomach couldn't take it – wouldn't know what to do with it. Same as that wool. That ain't a sweater till it's knitted. Now you crochet that wool into a chain' – and here he pulled a long crocheted chain of wool out of his pocket.

'Blimey, the man's a conjuror,' came the usual voice from the back. 'Where's the white rabbit, then?'

Sam pulled a white rabbit out of one of his pockets. It sat quietly on the table. There was a burst of clapping from the hall. Everyone turned to glare at the interrupter.

'As I was saying,' went on Sam. 'You get all these chemicals. Or nature does. It knits them together into long chains and you get amino acids. Long chains of amino acids – they make protein, like in this rabbit. Shorter chains – you get nuts and beans, or vegetable protein. Then you take purl and plain . . .' and yet another piece of knitting emerged from his enormous pockets. 'That's carbohydrates – starches, like bread and potatoes. And sugar, like demerara.

And then you get a bit of ribbing . . .' and once more he placed a piece of knitting in front of him. 'Now, that's fats. That's what makes up most of butter and marge. But that's only a beginning. 'Cos there's more. There's minerals. There's vitamins. And you've got to mix 'em, make 'em up.'

There was a startled silence as once more he delved into his pockets. He threw a handful of cotton reels and packets of needles on to the table.

'Vitamins,' he said. Buttons and buckles and laces came next. 'Minerals,' he said, 'what makes the whole thing work.'

Finally, from assorted pockets he pulled out a pair of pants, a white vest, a pair of blue jeans, a T-shirt with SAM IS THE GREATEST on it, and a pair of black plimsolls. He tossed them all up in the air.

'Is that all?' The voice from the back was just a little sarcastic.

'Can I have my boots back, please?' asked Bert.

'Can I have the rabbit?' asked Minty.

'All in good time,' said Sam. 'Now, are there any more questions?'

'Yes,' said Mrs Prendergast, rather nervously. 'It's about those vitamins.'

'Speak up', and 'I can't hear', came from the hall.

'Vitamins,' said Mrs Prendergast more boldly. 'I don't hold with them. All those pills. Waste of money, I call it.'

'I quite agree with you,' said Sam. 'Take Queen Victoria. She did all right, didn't she? How old was she when she died? Ninety something? And she never took a vitamin in her life . . .'

'There you are,' interrupted Mrs Prendergast, and she turned triumphantly to her neighbours. 'I told you so. What's all the fuss, then?'

'As I was saying,' went on Sam. 'She never took a vitamin in her life – not one that she *knew* of, 'cos they weren't discovered until 1915, by which time she was pushing up the daisies. Have you ever eaten an orange, or a lemon, or a grapefruit, Mrs P.?'

' 'Course I have,' retorted Mrs Prendergast.

'Vitamin C,' said Sam quickly. 'Anyone eaten carrots?'

Several hands went up.

'Vitamin A, or carotene, what makes vitamin A in your body. Anyone for peanuts, liver, pork?'

'Yes', and 'I like a bit of roast pork myself', came from the hall.

'Vitamin B,' said Sam. ' 'Course, there's lots of different B vitamins. Then there's D and E and K. Same thing. Vitamins are *in* food. Don't you worry, Mrs P., you eat all kinds of food – meat, fish, eggs, milk, green veg, fruit, bread, butter – you get your vitamins without any trouble.'

At this point Minty noticed that the rabbit was missing from the table.

'But what are they *for*, Sam?' Bert was asking.

'Like I told you, Bert,' said Sam. 'They're cotton or wool, or what you sew clothes with. They make it all work. Now, in your body, they're like messengers. They get around everywhere. Zoom, zoom. "Get cracking," they say, to your nerves and glands. Or, "Lie down and keep still for a bit," if they're overdoing it. All them minerals, too. They get the boot in, like. Keep you on the go. And now, are there any more questions?'

Silence in the hall. Everyone looked at everyone else. Except Minty. She looked at the rabbit, which was sitting on her lap.

'Well,' said Sam, taking a drink of water, 'there *is* something else which you can't do without. But I shall tell you about that in my next lecture, which is How to Climb Mount Everest. And now to conclude, I will give you a recipe. Does anyone know how to make a Swiss roll?'

'Push him down a mountain,' said a man at the back.

'Excellent, excellent,' said Sam. 'Same with an apple turnover, of course. Anyone know what is white, has just one horn, and gives milk?'

'A milk lorry,' said Bert. 'And can I have my boots back?'

So that was the end of the lecture. Bert got back his boots. Sam said Minty could keep the rabbit. The man at the back got his girlfriend to knit him a pair of socks, and Mrs P. went home determined to see if she could catch a glimpse of all those nasty vitamins that were infesting her nice food.

Food facts

Sugars and carbohydrates

Carbohydrates turn into sugars when they've been digested. They are in starchy foods, like bread, rice and potatoes. (Chew a piece of bread in your mouth. It will begin to taste sweet – that's the starch beginning to change into sugar.)

Sugars are burned in the body to produce energy. Sugar is in lots of food – mostly fruit, especially dried ones. We don't really need added sugar in our diet at all. It's one of the few foods which is a *pure* chemical, and doesn't contain vitamins, minerals, or anything else. So it's not a good idea to get hooked on sugar and sweet things. (Honey, though, *does* have small amounts of minerals in it.)

Proteins

There are two kinds – vegetable and animal. The animal ones have many more of the amino acids we need than vegetable ones. So if you are a vegetarian, you must eat a very wide range of vegetable protein.

It's the most important food. Every living cell needs protein. It's found in – especially – milk, cheese, eggs, meat. Also beans, peas and nuts. Peanuts have more than other nuts. Soya beans have the best mixture of vegetable amino acids.

Fats

These are obviously found in butter, margarine, oil, nuts and fatty meat. They give the body energy, and contain vitamins A, C, E and K.

Vitamins

There are about two dozen of these, but the most important are A, B, C, D and E.

Vitamin A was the first to be discovered, in 1915. It's found in milk, butter, margarine, liver, eggs and watercress. Yellow vegetables, especially carrots, have carotene in them, which turns into vitamin A inside you.

✳ If you don't get any vitamin A, you may suffer from 'night-blindness', which means your eyes can't adjust properly when you go out into the dark from a bright light inside.

Vitamin B – there are several of these. The main ones are now called riboflavin, thiamine and niacin. They're very important for proper growing, steady nerves and a good appetite. They're found especially in wheat germ, yeast, oranges and grapefruit, pork, oatmeal, peanuts and liver.

✳ When wheat and corn grains are manufactured into white flour and breakfast cereals like cornflakes, the wheat germ is removed. So by law, now, the vitamins have to be put back again.

Vitamin C was discovered in the 1930s. But way back in 1795, the British Navy had realized that lemons and limes had something in them which prevented scurvy. This was a disease which sailors on long journeys with no fresh fruit to eat used to get – it gives you sore gums, among other things. So lemon (or lime) juice was prescribed. That's why British sailors were called 'Limeys'.

It's found in citrus (sour, acid) fruits mostly, like oranges, lemons, grapefruit, blackcurrants and rosehips. And also in fresh green vegetables and in potatoes. It helps wounds to heal, and some people think it prevents colds and other illnesses. It's very important, anyway.

✳ In the West Indies there is a cherry called the 'acerola' which has thirty times as much vitamin C as an orange. You'd only need to eat one cherry a day.

Vitamin D is important because it helps the body to absorb calcium, to make teeth and bones. Otherwise, you get a bone disease called rickets, which used to be so common in England that it was called 'The English Disease'. Children used to wear braces to try and keep their bones straight.

Sunlight makes vitamin D in our bodies. It's also found especially in animal and fish livers – like cod-liver oil.

✳ The Eskimos never touch polar-bear's liver. They believe it to be poisonous. Experts found that it has so much vitamin D in it – a thousand times more than in fish livers – that it *is* harmful.

Vitamin E is still being investigated. It seems to act as a preservative in foods, and affects fertility in humans. It's in lots of foods – like wheat germ, most vegetables, eggs, liver and butter.

Minerals

All the following are in your body at this very moment: calcium, phosphorus, sulphur, sodium, chlorine, magnesium, iron, manganese, copper and iodine. That's in order of amount. Then there are tiny traces of: cobalt, fluorine, molybdenum, zinc and selenium.

Calcium is found in milk and fish bones (tinned sardines and salmon). Also in Rowntree's Fruit Gums! 99% of it goes into our teeth and bones, and to help the muscles contract and expand.

✳ If you put a frog's heart into a calcium solution, and then into a solution *without* calcium, you can make the heart stop and start beating again.

Phosphorus helps bones to grow properly. Marmite has a lot of it.

Sulphur is found in most proteins. Hair is 6% sulphur.

Iron is very important for making red corpuscles in the blood. (An adult has twenty-five million *times* a million red corpuscles in his body!) It's found especially in whole wheat and egg yolk, and also in dark green vegetables like spinach.

Roughage

This is the name given to plant fibre, which is composed of various kinds of cellulose. It doesn't necessarily *feel* rough when you eat it, but it's in fruit and vegetables, and in the outer covering of wheat grains, which is called bran. Human beings can't digest it, because we haven't got that sort of inside. But cows can, which is why they eat grass and we don't. It just goes through us, and people used to think it was no use at all. But now experts think it may be very important in preventing constipation and all sorts of other troubles in our intestines. (It absorbs water on the way through the intestines and maybe other substances too.) White flour does not have any bran in it. Wholewheat flour does.

Crazy cookery

To make crumbobblious cutlets, by Edward Lear

Procure some strips of beef, and having cut them into the smallest possible slices, proceed to cut them still smaller, eight, or perhaps nine times.

When the whole is thus minced, brush it up hastily with a new clothes-brush, and stir round rapidly and capriciously with a salt-spoon or soup-ladle.

Place the whole in a saucepan, and remove it to a sunny place – say, the roof of a house if free from sparrows or other birds – and leave it there for about a week.

At the end of that time, add a little lavender, some oil of almonds and a few herring-bones; and then cover the whole with four gallons of clarified crumbobblious sauce, when it will be ready for use.

Cut it into the shape of ordinary cutlets, and serve up in a clean tablecloth or dinner-napkin.

Food quiz 3
Who said?

1 'An army marches on its stomach.'
2 'Let them eat cake.'
3 'Look at Pork. There's a subject! If you want a subject, look at Pork!'
4 'Out, vile jelly!'
5 'How many strawberries grow in the sea?'
6 'Let me taste your ware.' (He was talking to a pieman.)

(Answers on page 154)

Who was it?

1 Who dined on mince, and slices of quince?
2 Who ate bread and honey in the parlour?
3 Who made some tarts all on a summer's day?
4 Who licked the platter clean?
5 Who sat in a corner eating a Christmas pie?
6 Who had white bread and butter for his supper?
7 Who burnt the cakes?
8 Who stole a piece of beef?
9 Who was made into a roly-poly pudding?
10 Who ate locusts and wild honey in the desert?

(Answers on page 154)

Sam Stubbins's celebrated free food lecture 6
How to climb Mount Everest

'Excuse me,' said Sam Stubbins, taking a large potato and a grater and a tumbler out of his bottom right-hand pocket. 'But I must have a drink.'

There was silence in the village hall as he took an empty bowl out of his top right-hand pocket. He grated the potato furiously into the bowl, and then poured off some juice into the tumbler. It was nearly full.

'That's better,' said Sam, taking a sip. 'Nothing like water.'

'Never touch the stuff if I can help it,' muttered Colonel Chumley-Mutt quietly.

But Sam heard him. 'Ah, but you can't help it, matey,' he said. 'Now, that potato – there was nearly a tumbler of water in that. And you, Colonel, beggin' your pardon, are awash with the stuff. You're more than half *made* of water, in fact. You're wet, if you don't mind my saying so.'

'Well ... I ... I ... didn't *think* I was ...' murmured the Colonel, rather bewildered.

'Don't worry,' said Sam. 'Everyone is. Got to be.'

'But why?' asked Minty, who felt sorry for the Colonel.

' 'Cos there isn't one cell in your body that can function without water. It's water what makes you go round. Otherwise you'd be a mummy. They'd put you in the British Museum straightaway, and people would pay to see you. 'Course, you wouldn't be able to see them, 'cos you'd be a goner. Anyone like a sweet, by the way?'

Sam threw handfuls of boiled sweets into the audience, and began sucking one himself. But then he realized he couldn't speak very well at the same time, so he crunched it up.

'Now,' Sam said, having hastily swallowed the sweet, 'your mouth's watering, right? That's the saliva. If your mouth was bone dry, that sweet'd just stay there for ever. But down it goes, into your stomach. That's one big watery mess, with digestive juices, acids, and stuff called bile. Then they get to work on that sweet, turning it into useful chemicals, digesting it. Then it takes a trip along the small intestine. That's quite a voyage, 'cos there's thirty feet of it, all neatly folded up inside you like a seaman's rope. It's like the bottom of a stagnant pool in there, all green and murky. That's the chyme—'

Here Sam paused, noticing that Mrs Prendergast had put her hands over her ears and was giving him one of her looks.

'There's water-weeds too,' he went on loudly, 'millions of them, in there. Little tiny things, less than a quarter of a millimetre long, sticking out from the sides. They're called *villi*, actually. And *they* absorb all the useful stuff from that sweet, and then it goes into the blood. That's all watery, too. And what you don't need of that sweet, goes into the large intestine and out the other end. Mission accomplished. And if there wasn't any water to wash all the wrong things out of your body, they'd never leave, and then you'd be in trouble!'

'Here,' said Bert. 'That's all very well. But what about climbing Mount Everest?'

'Ah yes,' said Sam. 'Now that was something, that was. What your real mountaineer always dreamed of doing. The highest mountain in the world. But they couldn't make it. They'd battle up through ice and snow, the old heart pounding away, lungs gasping, frostbite gnawing the fingers and toes, all set for the last dash to the top. And they couldn't do it. Not till Sir Edmund Hillary and Sherpa Tenzing came along. Know what they did? They took special stoves and fuel with them, right to the top camp, so as their party could melt the snow and have five or six pints of water to drink every day. Now, there was a Swiss party, what tried to get up there, they only had less than *one* pint of water each a day. They never made it. Now, they do say that it may have been that extra water that helped the British team to get the flag on top of the world at last. 'Cos, you climb, and you sweat, and you use up all that energy, and if you don't have enough water, then you just ain't no good. Like I said, it's water what makes you go round – or up, as the case may be.'

'Can you drink *too much* of it?' asked Minty.

'Well,' said Sam, ' 'course, if you take in *anything*, food or water, that's more than you actually need, then it stays around, puts on weight. But mostly, you sweat it off, or it comes out the other end all right. 'Course, there was the little pig that drank too much. Heard about him?'

'No.'

'Well, this little pig went into a pub, and ordered himself five lemonades, six Cokes, a glass of iced water and three pints of beer. Another little pig that was sitting up at the bar, sipping a double whisky, said to him: "Isn't that too much for a little pig like you?" And the little pig answered: "But I'm the little piggy that went wee, wee, wee, all the way home." '

Mrs Prendergast, who had dared to take her hands off her ears, didn't approve of that story at all. She clapped her hands back on again, not realizing that was the end of the lecture. But she wasn't going to risk being shocked again, so she just sat there, and took no notice of Sam shouting and waving his arms, telling her to go. Finally, he turned a cartwheel, and disappeared off the side of the platform. The Colonel came up then, and offered Mrs P. his arm, and together they left the hall.

How much water is there in food?

milk – 87%
an egg – 73%
beefsteak – about 55%
pork sausage – 50%
fried cod in batter – 63%
apple – 84%
banana – 71%
gooseberry and grapefruit – 90%
melon – 94%
rhubarb – 95·5%
peanut – 4·5%
tin of baked beans – 69·6%
potato chip – 47%
Mars bar – 6·9%

✳ A newborn baby is 75% water.

✳ Lack of water is one of the worries during space flights. On one of the Mercury flights, Astronaut Cooper lost a lot of weight, and became dehydrated; so after that they have to take special care to see that all astronauts get enough water.

✳ Why can a camel go for a long time without any water? A camel's hump isn't filled with water. It's a big, fatty lump. Now, when the camel goes on a long journey, the fat gets burned up to give energy. And it's the water that gets released from this fat after it's burned that keeps the camel going. He doesn't lose it in perspiration like we would, because he has fine hairs all over his body. So the water stays inside and the camel doesn't feel thirsty. You can actually see that a camel's hump is much smaller by the end of a long journey.

✳ Read all about it – in *How to Cross the Sahara Safely*, by Mustapha Camel.

How long does it take to digest food?

apple – $1\frac{1}{2}$ hours
milk – 2 hours
boiled egg – 3 hours
boiled potato – $3\frac{1}{2}$ hours
butter – $3\frac{1}{2}$ hours
cheese – $3\frac{1}{2}$ hours
fried beefsteak – 4 hours
roast pork – $4\frac{1}{4}$ hours

✳ Fatty foods and fried things take a long time to leave the stomach. That's why you feel fuller after eating them, and for longer. Bacon and eggs for breakfast, for instance, stick around much longer than cornflakes.

How to grow banknotes and hatch Americans

Some food legends are very old. Like the Turkish legend that when the Devil was sent out of Paradise and first set foot on earth, an onion grew where he put his right foot, and a garlic plant where he put his left. Or like the Eastern legend about jade, which is a very hard, greenish precious stone. If you powdered it and ate it, they said, you would live for a thousand years, become invisible, or fly through the air.

The Samoans believe that their people used to eat a herb which made them able to drink seawater. And in those days they went on long, long sea journeys, to places as far away as New Zealand. But the secret is lost, and the herb cannot be found any more.

Another old legend is about not leaving any food on your plate. If your enemy gets hold of your leftover food, then he can cast a spell on it, which will work against you.

And there's an old story about making butter. One day, three frogs fell into a huge vat of milk. They all swam around for a while, and then two of them gave up and were drowned. But the *third* frog

kept on going, round and round, legs up and down, churning up the milk. And gradually the milk turned into butter. The frog was able to stand high and dry on the butter, and jump out! (Moral: **never give up.**)

There are newer legends, too. In the Second World War and afterwards, the Americans and Australians arrived in New Guinea. They were mostly soldiers and government officials. And with them came supplies – tinned foods, soap, ammunition, radio sets. Sometimes these came by boat, sometimes by submarine. Now, the Tolai tribe that lived there watched it all. They observed the soldiers in their little huts, twiddling the knobs of their radio transmitters. They observed that after this, the boats came, laden with goods. So they began to think. And gradually a new legend, the Cargo Cult, grew up.

So the tribesmen burnt their crops and killed their animals, because the white man managed without them. They fixed up their own radio transmitters, and for weeks on end they would crouch over them, like the white man, twiddling the knobs. Their leader did ritual dances round the transmitter, poking it, inspiring it. And the people waited. And waited. But the submarines never came to them.

Because the radio was only an old packing-case, and the knobs and dials were only painted on.

And one day, they saw an advertisement in one of the white man's papers. There was a picture of a tree with banknotes growing on it. (The advertisement was for a bank, to encourage savings.) Anyway, the Tolai were entranced with the idea of this money tree. They collected hundreds of coins and buried them, and waited for them to grow . . .

While over in New Britain, just after the war, there was a chief who had an egg. Just an ordinary hen's egg. But he watched over it very carefully, because an American soldier was growing in that egg, and on hatching day, he would rule the tribe and supply them with good things.

✳ It's easy to make butter, by the way, *without* a frog. Pour off the cream from the top of a pint of milk. Put the cream into a large jar with a top – a jam jar is fine – then shake gently. Shake, shake, shake. Soon blobs of solid yellow will appear, surrounded by white liquid. When the liquid has gone quite pale, pour it off into a bowl. Turn out the solid part. Add a little salt. Beat it, and shape it with a pair of wooden spoons, and there's your butter. If you use the cream from one pint of Gold Top milk, you'll get enough butter to put on your bread for tea. With less creamy milk, use the cream off two pints to make a decent amount of butter.

How to find a husband

In the West of England, the girls used to gather crab-apples, and lay them up in the attics, in the initials of their boyfriends. Then they waited. On Michaelmas Day they would clamber up and see how the apples had lasted. Those that had lasted best would show the initials of the best husband to choose.

And if you want to dream of your future husband, peel some onions and put them under your pillow on St Thomas's Day, 21 December.

The story of simnel cake

Simnel cake is eaten at Easter time. You can buy it nowadays; here is an old story about how it was first made.

Once upon a time, there was an old couple; the old man was called Simon, and the old woman was called Nelly. Now, one day, the children came round, asking for cakes, but poor Simon and Nelly had nothing in the way of cakes except a piece of old dough and the remains of a Christmas pudding.

'What shall we do?' said Simon to Nelly.

'Put the pudding in the dough, and bake it.'

'Boil it, you mean.'

'It should be baked.'

'Don't be silly – boil the thing.'

'It must be baked.'

Well, the bake/boil argument went from bad to worse, until Simon and Nelly stopped talking and started to throw furniture at each other. Nelly threw a stool at Simon, which broke against the wall. Simon wasn't a good shot either. He threw a broom at Nelly and missed. She threw back a couple of eggs . . .

There's nothing like a good fight for bringing a married couple together again. After a while, they got the broken wood together and lit the stove. Then they put the pudding in the dough. They boiled it and *then* baked it. And they used the broken eggs to glaze the top. So the cake they invented was called the Sim-Nell cake, after both of them. And the simnel cake lived happily ever afterwards. (Nowadays it usually has marzipan round the outside.)

Food of the gods

Nectar

Nectar was the legendary drink of the gods. It came from the honey that flowers make. Perhaps it tasted rather like mead, which is a drink made from bees' honey.

Ambrosia

Ambrosia was the favourite food of the gods. No one knows for sure just what it was, as there aren't any gods about to give the recipe. It may have been made from the *amanita muscaria*, which is a very dangerous kind of mushroom that gives hallucinations. They may have mixed the juice with milk, water, herbs or alcohol – or even spruce-beer, which is very powerful stuff. The word 'ambrose' in English means 'wood-sage', which has a lovely smell. Perhaps that was used to flavour it. It must have been something very strong, anyway.

Apples

Apples were very magical things, real food for the gods. The old Norse legends say that Idun, the daughter of Odin, kept some golden apples locked up in a golden casket. Every day she gave each god one apple. And that is why they never grow old.

The daughters of Atlas, who were called the Hesperides, had a Garden, in which a most precious tree grew. This bore golden apples, too, and there was a dragon always coiled round the foot of the tree, to guard the wonderful fruit. This dragon had a hundred heads and several voices. Eventually, Hercules came and killed the dragon and picked the golden apples off the tree. (Some people think these 'golden apples' may have been quinces.)

An apple a day, Sends the doctor away.	Roast apple at night, Starves the doctor outright.
Apple in the morning, Doctor's warning.	Eat an apple going to bed, Knock the doctor on the head.

✱ **Eggs** are very magical things, too. Some people won't touch them because they are the very beginning of life. Anyway, if you do eat a boiled egg, you *must* break up the shell completely – otherwise witches will come and make the shell into a boat.

Sam Stubbins's celebrated free food lecture 7
The case of the salted peanut

Sam and his overcoat strode on to the platform. Putting his watch on the table, he said, 'I shall speak for exactly one hour tonight. Now, how many people are here?'

There were so few that he kept the number to himself.

'Now,' he went on, undeterred, 'tonight there will be no chucking food around – it's a disgusting habit and a waste . . .'

'Quite right,' said Mrs Prendergast.

'And besides, I have to clear it all up,' Sam added. 'So, catch, will you?' He threw handfuls of salted peanuts into the audience. 'One half each,' he ordered. 'Just one. And hang on to it. I'll tell you when you can eat it. Now, are you all sitting comfortably?'

The Colonel was still scrabbling on the floor, searching for his nut.

'Tell me, Colonel,' said Sam. 'What do you do when you wake up in the morning?'

'Well . . . um . . . I . . . er . . .' stammered the Colonel. 'I just lie there for a bit, not doing anything, really. Thinking, of course,' he added.

'Of course,' said Sam. 'Nerving yourself to take the plunge, like? Getting into gear? Otherwise, just sort of ticking over? Same here. In and out go the old lungs, lub-dub, goes the heart, seventy times a minute. In–out, in–out, that's the muscles that makes them go. Breathing in oxygen, pumping it round all those miles of veins, burning it up in the cells, turning it into carbon dioxide. Where's the carbon come from? All that food you ate the night before. And then breathing out all that gas. The cells busy all over the body. That's basal metabolism. Just ticking over, like I said.'

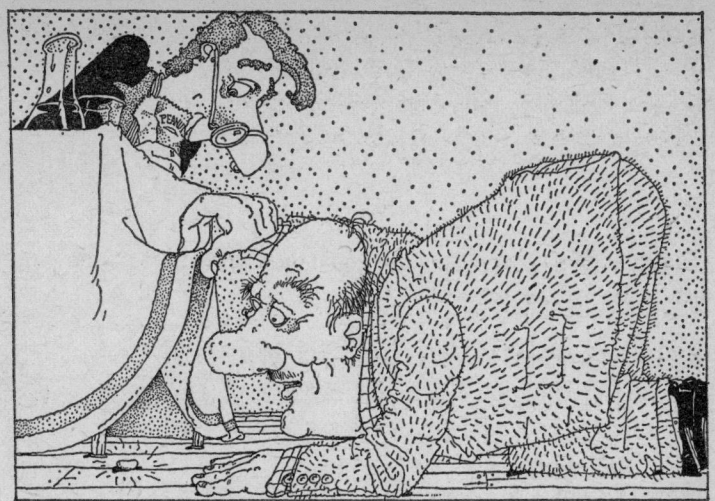

'Basin of what?' asked Mollie Pratt, puzzled.

'Basal metabolism,' said Sam. ' "Metabolism" means the things that happen inside you, just to keep you going. And *basal* metabolism, that's the very least you do, when you're lying still and quiet. D'you ever feel hot, Colonel, with all that burning going on?'

'Well, not hot exactly. But the bed's nice and warm. I didn't know I was *burning*,' said the Colonel, looking rather worried.

'You ain't on fire, Colonel. Don't worry. It's all chemical changes going on – not flames and smoke. Lucky, that. It's all happening at 98·4 degrees, or you'd be charcoal biscuit in the morning. But if you was to lie still like that all day, you'd use up 1,700 calories.'

'What *are* calories?' asked Bert. 'I've never understood.'

'Just a measurement of heat, Bert, that's all,' replied Sam. 'If you was shut up in a glass cage with a pile of ice, like a bloke called Lavoisier once did to a guinea-pig, then you'd melt it. You'd raise the temperature, like, with all that heat your breathing and burning makes inside you, and turn the ice to water. Then you measure. How much carbon's got to be burnt to heat the ice? You take some food, which is mostly carbon, and burn it in oxygen. And the amount of food that's got to be burnt to raise one gramme of water by one degree – that's a calorie. Now Minty, what do you do when you get up in the morning?'

'She rushes round like a scalded cat,' said Minty's mother, before Minty could get a word in. ' 'Cos she's going to be late for school!'

'Aha,' said Sam. 'That's it. Best way to keep the weight down. You belt up and down stairs, can't find your clothes, lose your games kit, get all steamed up, your muscles hard at work, burning up calories. Best way to get an appetite for breakfast – 'cos you've got to replace all that energy.'

'But if *all* food has got calories,' said the Colonel, slowly thinking it out, 'does it matter *what* you eat? It must be all the same in the end.'

Sam delved into one of his pockets and brought out a paper bag. He solemnly handed it down to Bert, and said, 'Doughnuts. Lots of calories. Bags of them. Enough calories for the whole day, considering the amount of work you do. Now, that's your calorie-controlled diet for the day.'

And then Sam began taking off his clothes. He laid his overcoat gently on the table, on account of all the things still in the pockets. He took off his tie, then his shirt, then his shoes and socks . . . saying to Bert meanwhile: 'D'you think that's a good diet?'

'Well, you *said* it was all the calories I needed,' Bert said, rather doubtfully. Actually, he couldn't think of a nicer diet, being keener on doughnuts than almost anything else in the world. But he had a sneaking suspicion he was being got at. I mean, it couldn't be right, surely? But why not?

Sam went on stripping. He was just about to undo his trousers, when Mrs Prendergast stood up, and declared, 'I did *not* come here to see a disgusting exhibition of nudity.'

'Nothing disgusting about nudity,' said Sam, who was extremely proud of his figure. Still, he could see from the look in Mrs P.'s eye that he was going too far, as usual. 'I was just demonstrating a doughnut diet, that's all.'

'What *do* you mean?' asked Mrs P.

'Well,' said Sam. 'Supposing I went around all day, summer and winter, in my vest and pants. I'd look a right Charlie sitting behind my desk at the office. And I'd get a shocking cold in winter. Same with these doughnuts. You'd be missing something, like trousers and shoes and coats. 'Cos doughnuts are short on protein, and vitamins, and minerals. *I'd* get dirty looks and pneumonia, and Bert'd get malnutrition. That's not getting the right food. You've got to have the right amount of calories to use up, sure enough, but you've got to have the right mixture of food, too.'

'But supposing you eat *more* calories than you need?' asked Minty, who was on the plump side.

'You get fat,' said Sam.

There was a pause. Sam buttoned up his shirt and began putting on his tie.

'But surely, everything doesn't make you fat?' asked Minty, not liking Sam's answer one bit.

'Everything,' said Sam firmly. 'If you've got more food inside you than you use, then it turns into fat. 'Course, if you want to swim the Channel, that's a good idea. You thinking of doing that?'

'No,' said Minty. 'Not at the moment, anyway.'

'Pity,' said Sam. 'You'd be just right. You'd have a nice layer of fat, to keep you warm. Like a dolphin. Know why the dinosaurs died out, by the way? They was too big. Couldn't run about the place. It's a terrible strain, carrying all that extra load of fat about all day. Ever seen a seal on land? They ain't very nimble. So if you've got extra weight, you'd better lose it. There was this little boy, his mother asked him what he was going to do when he grew as big as his daddy. "Go on a diet," he said. And quite right, too.'

'But how?' asked Minty.

'Best thing to do,' said Sam, 'is cut out the food what gives you the least things, like sugar. Sugar's a pure chemical. It *only* gives you energy, nothing else – no vitamins, no minerals, no body-building stuff at all. There's not many things you eat that only does that. Then there's fats – cream and butter have more calories than meat or veg, so cut down on those, too, and you'll be OK. Now, any more questions?'

Silence. Sam looked at his watch. 'Right,' he said. 'The hour's up. You may eat your peanut.'

Minty, Steve and Mollie Pratt looked rather embarrassed. They'd eaten theirs long ago.

'That's to replace all the calories you've used up sitting and listening to me,' said Sam. ' 'Course, Mrs P., you could have an extra nibble, on account of your standing up and getting into a stew. But that's all the rest of you need – half a salted peanut. Mustn't overdo it, you know. 'Course, *I've* been busier,' he went on, pulling a chicken leg out of a pocket. 'Got to keep my strength up. It's hard work being a Celebrated Food Lecturer,' and he munched away.

✳ *Fried* foods have lots more calories than plain foods.
✳ We in this country eat 600,000 tons of sweets per year – almost as much as the weight of the entire population of London!
✳ We each eat fifty tons of food in a lifetime.
✳ 25% of all the people in America are thought to be overweight, and 44% of infants in the Midlands of England are too heavy, as well.
✳ We are lightest in July and heaviest in January.
✳ The heaviest man in England is George Mackeree. He weighs 244·48 kg (38 st 7 lbs).

How many grammes of sugar in some foods

1 flat teaspoonful of sugar – 5
1 dessertspoonful of jam – 5
50 gr (2 oz) of chocolate – 30

1 bottle of Cola – 12
25 gr (1 oz) of sweets – 20
50 gr (2 oz) of ice-cream – 12

A greedy young fellow of Crediton,
Took one pound of cream and spread it on
  A chocolate biscuit,
    Then murmured, 'I'll risk it.'
His tomb bears the date that he said it on.

How many calories in some foods

1 almond – 8
1 medium apple – 70
1 banana – 95
1 boiled egg – 80

1 potato – 105
1 shredded wheat – 100
1 chicken leg – 90

Calories per 25 gr (1 oz) of food

Mars bar – 127   peanuts – 171
Marmite – 2   lean beef – 62
doughnut – 101   butter – 226
treacle tart – 107

Fried food goes shooting up in calories, because the fat goes into whatever you fry.

1 fried egg has 135 calories: 1 boiled egg has 80
1 fried mushroom has 217: 1 raw mushroom has 7
1 fried onion has 355: 1 raw onion has 28

✳ $2\frac{1}{4}$ kg (5 lbs) of cooked rice has the same number of calories as 340 gr (12 oz) of fat.

✳ Frogs' legs have 82 calories for every 100 gr ($\frac{1}{4}$ lb) – and contain quite a lot of protein and iron.

✳ Caviar has 16 calories for every tablespoonful.

✳ You probably need about 2,500 calories per day.

Calories used up in doing things

Everyone is different. Adults use fewer calories than children, doing the same things. (Maybe they do things less energetically?) Boys use up more calories than girls. It depends on how old you are, and what you weigh.

Take *cycling*:
Boys aged 9–11 use up 5·12 calories per hour for every kilogramme they weigh.
Boys aged 12–14 use up 4·47.
Girls aged 9–11 use up 4·93.
Girls aged 12–14 use up 3·74.

(They found this out by having children do all sorts of different things, with rubber pipes clipped to their noses, and haversacks with oxygen on their backs, and pipes in their mouths – all measuring how much oxygen they took in, and how much carbon dioxide they breathed out.)

Anyway, to give you a rough idea, here is the amount of calories that a boy aged 9–11, weighing about 37 kg (5 st 12 lbs) would use up doing different things.

Calories used up per hour
cycling – 185
eating – 80
listening to radio – 75
standing and singing – 85
roller skating – 225
dressing – 153
walking at 2 mph – 140
walking at 3 mph – 205
washing up – 105

Calories used up per minute
climbing stairs – 7
running – 11
walking at 4 mph – 6

✳ If you are sitting still, working very hard at maths homework or something like that, you would use up the same calories (on top of your basal metabolism) as there are in *one half of a salted peanut*!

✳ But if you were playing football for an hour, you'd need about a bag of them.

✳ A man climbing Mount Everest would use up $14\frac{1}{2}$ calories per minute.

Desperate diets

One year on 24 June, a man called Dr William Stark began a diet. He wanted to see just how few things he could manage to live on. So he started on just bread and water.

26 July – he allowed himself some sugar.

11 August – he noticed he had ulcers, swelling gums, and his right nostril had gone bright red. In other words, he had scurvy. He went on, but added olive oil to his diet.

6 September – he could hardly walk. So he changed to bread, water and milk. He still felt pretty groggy; so eventually he added some boiled beef, and then some honey and rosemary tea. Finally, he reduced his diet to bread, Cheshire cheese and rosemary tea.

18 February, the next year – he gave up the cheese.

23 February – he gave up the ghost and died, after eight months of dieting.

Saint Hilarian was supposed to have lived
for three years on   – half a pint of lentils a day, with cold water
then three years on – dry bread and salt and water
then three years on – wild herbs and raw roots of shrubs
then three years on – barley bread and lightly cooked vegetables
Then he added oil to this diet and lived –
until he was eighty!

Dad's Army diet

It's 1943. There's a war on – World War II. German submarines are lurking in the Channel like big black killer whales. Out in the Atlantic, too, they are silently prowling, waiting to strike. Every ship is packed with soldiers, for the war effort. There's not much room for food, because – remember – **there's a war on.**

Back home, there are the posters – **Dig for victory. Walls have ears.** There's sticky tape crisscrossed on the windowpanes, to hold the glass together when the bombs blast. No light in the streets at night. Every curtain is lined with blackout material, so that not a chink of light can escape. (The Warden will be after you if it does.) Even bicycle lamps are half-covered with black paper, so the light doesn't shine up in the sky and show the enemy planes where the towns are. There's hardly any petrol. No going on holiday. **Is your journey really necessary?**

And down at Warmington-on-Sea, Corporal Jones is hiding a few pounds of sausages under the counter for favoured customers, and even a bit of liver too, and maybe a heart. Because they are off the ration, and there's only one shilling's worth of meat each – for a week. And what's Private Walker up to? He's out buying sugar from the Americans to flog to the Warden. (Sugar ration: eight ounces – two hundred grammes – per week.)

And Mrs Mainwaring is trying to find something for Captain Mainwaring's breakfast. She's a bit slow, as usual. And he's stomping round the kitchen, saying, 'Hurry up, woman,' and fuming about being late at the bank, and what will Wilson think?

Poor Mrs Mainwaring. What can she give him? Cornflakes? They're rationed, and the packet was finished yesterday. And there's not much milk anyway, at only half a pint a day. Toast and butter and marmalade? But there's only two ounces (fifty grammes) of butter for the whole week, that's the ration, and it all disappeared yesterday at tea. A boiled egg? Pity – they've eaten this week's egg. Got to wait till next Tuesday for another . . .

It all sounds crazy, now. But in 1943, every single food, except bread, flour, potatoes, fresh vegetables and some fruit, and fish, is rationed. That means – meat, bacon, cheese, fats of all kinds, sugar, jam, tea, tinned meats, tinned fish, beans, tinned and dried fruit, rice, cereals, biscuits, syrup, treacle, chocolate, sweets, milk, eggs and oranges are all rationed in one way or another. And some things you just can't get at all.

Rationing started in 1940, and some foods were still rationed in 1954. So if you were eight years old in 1940, you couldn't eat just what you liked till you were twenty-two!

It began with basic foods in 1940 – tea, sugar, bacon and ham, butter and other fats, and meat. You had your ration – so much every week, and that was that. Once the shopkeeper had cut the

MEAT	36	35	34	33	32	31	30	29	28	27	26	25
		9				8				7		
*Surname and Initials												
EGGS	36	35	34	33	32	31	30	29	28	27	26	25
		9				8				7		
*Surname and Initials												
FATS	36	35	34	33	32	31	30	29	28	27	26	25
		9				8				7		
*Surname and Initials												
CHEESE	36	35	34	33	32	31	30	29	28	27	26	25
		9				8				7		
*Surname and Initials												
BACON	36	35	34	33	32	31	30	29	28	27	26	25
		9				8				7		
*Surname and Initials												
SUGAR	36	35	34	33	32	31	30	29	28	27	26	25
		9				8				7		
	S	R	Q	P	S	R	Q	P	S	R	Q	P
*Surname and Initials												

little square for the week out of your ration book, then you'd had whatever it was for the week.

Later, other things came on the ration – cheese, chocolates and biscuits, and all the other foods I listed before. The chocolate and sweet coupons had a special name – they were called Personal Points. Sometimes the rations were a bit more, and sometimes they were a bit less. Meat was mostly about a shilling's worth a week, but sometimes it went up by twopence, or even fourpence. Cheese was mostly one to three ounces (twenty-five to seventy-five grammes) a week, but for six months in 1942 it actually went up to eight ounces (two hundred grammes)!

The ordinary sweet and chocolate ration was three ounces (seventy-five grammes) a week; but at Christmas in 1944, children were allowed eight ounces (two hundred grammes). And they were allowed oranges, too, when there were any. Soap was on the ration,

16

Food Office Code No. as on front cover [   ]

Surname and Initials...

This page may be detached and used by itself after period 6 but, if you do detach it, you should fill in details above.

E13	E13	E13	E13	D13	D13	D13	D13
E12	E12	E12	E12	D12	D12	D12	D12
E11	E11	E11	E11	D11	D11	D11	D11
E10	E10	E10	E10	D10	D10	D10	D10
E9	E9	E9	E9	D9	D9	D9	D9
E8	E8	E8	E8	D8	D8	D8	D8
E7	E7	E7	E7	D7	D7	D7	D7

too. Chimney sweeps (even part-time chimney sweeps), coalminers and children under two got a bigger ration of soap. (If you were over two, then presumably the government supposed you were naturally clean, or didn't like washing, because you got the same as ordinary adults.)

All through the war the rationing went on. And then the war ended, but the rationing didn't. It went on and on. Some things that hadn't been rationed during the war, began to be, after the war ended. Jellies were rationed in 1946, till 1950. And bread began to be rationed too, in 1946, for two years. The amount of bread you were allowed varied, 'according to age and what you did for a living. If you were a manual worker, you got more than other people. If you were ten years old, you could get two large loaves and a bun a week. But if you were eleven, then you had three large loaves and a bun. (There wasn't very much white flour about, by the way, so bread tended to be off-white.)

Ice-cream was very scarce, and there were **no bananas** from 1940 to 1946 for anyone. There just wasn't a banana to be seen in the shops at all. So some children of six years old had never seen a banana in their lives! They were so rare, that at the end of the war, one was auctioned for £35. But after 1946, there were some bananas to be had, though until 1950 they were only for children under eighteen, or people over seventy.

Still, it wasn't all bad. People had other things to eat – like whale-meat stew, which some said was delicious and some said tasted fishy. And there was a strange fish called *snoek*. And dried eggs, if you were lucky. And someone discovered that grated carrots made a rich, dark looking Christmas pudding, if you hadn't any currants. And the government issued all sorts of recipes, to help people make the best of things – like the recipe for roast potatoes, which they said were so delicious you didn't need any meat to go with them.

And the Americans, with their Lend–Lease programme, sent over all sorts of foods – like the very strong, bitter orange jelly which always turned up with rice pudding at school dinners. There was Spam and sliced peaches, too, and very many other things, which helped to fill the shelves. You *could* buy them, but they were still rationed, too, on a points system, so one week you might have to decide to have a tin of Spam *or* a tin of sliced peaches, because your ration book wouldn't run to both.

But, as far as I know, no one really suffered, and no one went really hungry, because of rationing. (It was the mothers who had the really difficult time, with all that managing to do.) And there was a lot of busy digging of allotments and garden patches, and keeping of hens and rabbits. Which is not a bad idea, even without a war. I wonder if Mrs Mainwaring kept chickens. No, I'm sure she didn't. But maybe Captain Mainwaring would do a bit of digging in his spare time, which is probably why he always looked a bit stiff on parade. And as for Sergeant Wilson – well, I'm sure Mrs Pike saw *he* didn't lack for anything.

And if food gets really scarce . . .

. . . here are some 'recipes' suggested in *Punch* (31 October 1973).

Artichauts vinaigrettes (serves 4)
4 tennis balls
1 small privet hedge
1 bottle Gloy
seasoning
water (if available)

Shave the tennis balls. Strip the privet leaves, setting the twigs aside (they make excellent crudités), and gum them to the bald tennis balls

with the Gloy. Dip in the water, if you have any; there is no need to boil, since this squanders energy, and it would make no difference anyhow; but a bit of gleam on the leaves is most effective. Season with anything you have to hand; floor-grit does very well as black pepper, and feels quite authentic on the teeth. Soak a piece of newspaper in vinegar and hang it near a lightbulb in the room you plan to eat in.

A tip: you may find that, the guests having eaten the leaves, they will wish to attack the artichoke hearts with a knife and fork, which may result in embarrassing bouncing. If, however, you carefully section the balls beforehand into handy mouth-sized pieces, this may be obviated. *Another tip*: even after shaving, you may find that the manufacturer's name is still legible on the skin. Remember to remove this with bleach; it is presuming too far on your guests' good manners to expect them to tuck into an artichoke marked Slazenger.

Oysters (serves 4)
24 small ashtrays
1 jar Vaseline
water

Very little compares with the classic simplicity of the oyster, unfortunately. However: take the ashtrays, fill to the brim with cold water, and spoon a blob of Vaseline into each tiny pool. *A tip*: be sure to clean the shells carefully. A pearl is one thing, an old dog-end quite another.

Melon

1 rugger ball (Honeydew)
1 soccer ball (Ogen)
1 packet blancmange
1 pail
1 stirrup pump

Everyone likes melon; or did. Take the ball, according to preference, mix the blancmange mixture in the pail, and fill the ball with the stirrup pump. Allow to set, paint green or yellow, section, remove stitches, and serve. *A tip*: pips lend a matchless touch of authenticity, especially when agglomerated in that delicious pulpy jelly. So if it's late March, and you have that net still handy . . .

✱ **News item** In 1973, a health-food addict was in the habit of drinking up to eight pints of carrot juice per day. He turned bright yellow and died of vitamin A poisoning. (Carrots are an important source of vitamin A – but you can have too much of a good thing.)

There was a young lady of Lynn,
Who was so uncommonly thin,
   That when she essayed,
   To drink lemonade,
She slipped through the straw and fell in.

There was an old person of Dean,
Who dined on one pea and a bean,
   For he said, 'More than that
   Would make me too fat,
And I desperately want to be lean.'

✳ And talking of lean people:
'There never was much to him, he's no more than a rasher of wind and a fried snowball.'
'She's that thin, you could pull her through a flute backwards and it wouldna stop the playing.'
'He's as fat as a matchstick with the wood shaved off.'

✳ Definition of a fat man: Food gone to waist.

Sam Stubbins's celebrated free food lecture 8

How to live to be a hundred

'The first thing to do,' said Sam, 'is to find a place about three thousand feet up with a nice warm climate. No towns, no factories, just fields. You have lots of children and you live a peaceful life, never getting into trouble—' here he paused because Mrs Prendergast was getting up out of her seat.

'No hurry, Mrs P.,' he called. 'You've got another forty years to go. There's a slow boat leaving *after* the lecture, if you don't mind.'

But Mrs Prendergast had only lost her glasses.

'No drinking or smoking, I suppose,' remarked Colonel Chumley-Mutt, sadly.

'Funny, that,' said Sam. 'Now, there's lots of people in Georgia, that's in Southern Russia, who live in just the sort of place I was telling you about. There's two thousand of them, so they say, who're over a hundred years old. There's Vanno Djachiadzi, for instance. He's 140. Now he gave up smoking when he was 110. Says he's a non-drinker, 'cos he doesn't drink any grape-vodka, which is the local knock-out drink. He just drinks two bottles of wine a day, that's all.'

'Sounds an OK sort of life,' said a voice.

'Great,' said Sam. 'All you do is work out in the fields very hard all your life. And you don't stop. No retiring till maybe you're 120.'

'Knew there was a catch somewhere,' said the same voice.

'Jolly good show,' said the Colonel.

'There's one fellow there,' went on Sam, 'called Astan Shlarba. He's a farmer and a horse-tamer. He's 123 and his son is fifty. And there's another bloke, called Senat, who strides around his village wearing a long goat-hair cloak. He's 120, he's got fifty people in his family and a son who's ninety-five.'

'I don't believe it,' called Bert Jenkins.

'We-e-ll,' said Sam. 'Trouble is, they've got no birth certificates. They just remember things. Like Vanno – he remembers some great scandal, way back in 1837. Now maybe he does. Maybe someone told him about it. But if you've got a son who's ninety-five, you've got to be pretty old yourself. Anyway, they're being investigated. And their food. 'Cos that's important. Now, some of them are vegetarians and some of them aren't. But they all eat lots of fresh fruit and vegetables, with lots of spices. They may eat a goat on special occasions, and chickens. And they have a doughy sort of bread made out of maize. You roll it up and dip it in strong garlic and pepper sauce. Reckon that keeps the system nicely tuned up. All that drink, too. But they never seem to get *drunk* much. They can take it. Could be all that hard open-air work.'

'What about the women?' called Mollie Pratt.

'Well,' said Sam, 'they don't smoke or drink. But then, they don't live nearly so long.'

'It's all those children, I expect,' said Mollie. 'Takes it out of you.'

' 'Course, Georgia isn't the only place where people live so long,' went on Sam. 'There's a valley way up in the Andes, in Ecuador, called the Valley of Paradise. Now that's a strange place. There's fifteen people over a hundred there in just one little village. They've got a factory. It makes rum from sugar cane – 110° proof, which is nearly twice as strong as whisky. They all drink three cupfuls a day, too. And know what their main crop is? Tobacco. Now, the village baker there is a woman, and she's 103. She works ten hours a day at that, and the rest of the time in the fields. And she breeds guinea-pigs in her spare time. And there's Miguel – he's 127. He *is* retired, actually. Gave up working when he was 125. Reckon he thought his children could keep him in his old age. He's got ninety-eight grand-children and seventy-eight great-grandchildren.'

'I don't believe it,' called Bert Jenkins again. 'Someone's been kidding you.'

'Not at all,' said Sam. 'They've all been christened. And their names and dates got written down in the church books. There's Gabriel Sanchez, too, he's 130. He climbs a mountain every day to hoe his fields. They do say they've got such powerful calf muscles from all that climbing, that those muscles help their hearts by pumping the blood round too. Sort of a helping leg, like.' (Groans from the audience.)

'Now,' went on Sam, barely acknowledging the reception, 'they mostly live on fruit and veg too. And a bit of goat-meat occasion-

ally, like the geezers in Georgia. But no one knows for sure how they do it. There are two rivers down in the valley – could be there's some good minerals in that water, what stop them ageing. Not that they're a clean lot, though. They're filthy. Doesn't seem to make any difference, though. But they are a peaceable lot, like the Georgians. Same way of life, really. There are two policemen who roam around a lot of villages, and they're dying of boredom. Nothing to do. They did have a case once. There was a woman arrested for saying nasty things about other people. But that was it. And no heart attacks, ulcers or mental illness. Reckon you could say they were a happy lot of old hard-working skellingtons.'

'But what about other places?' asked Minty.

'Same thing in the Himalayas,' replied Sam. 'They live mostly on apricots, vegetables and goat's milk, with a spot of the old goat on feast days. They live for ages. 'Course, in Bulgaria and places like that, they say it's yoghurt that keeps them young. Now, there *was* a bloke called Sylvester Magee, out in Columbia, Missouri. He was supposed to be 130 when he died, and wounded twice in the American Civil War. But just the other day, Mrs Polly Mason died in Louisiana. She was born a slave, and lived to be 118. Said she lived so long on a diet of red beans and rice, chewing tobacco and drinking a quart of corn liquor a day.'

'I say,' said the Colonel. 'That's going it a bit, what? But what about long-livers in England?'

''Course, there are people over a hundred here, too,' said Sam. 'But not so many, when you think of all the population. Lucky, really, for the Queen. Now, when you're a hundred, you send your birth certificate to the Queen and she sends you a telegram. Very nice, and doesn't take up too much of her time. Now, if she was Queen of Georgia, she'd be popping down to the post office every other hour of the day. And anyway, the oldest person in England is only 112. 'Course, there was the Countess Desmond...' Sam paused. 'She was supposed to be 140 when she died in 1732. She fell out of an apple tree. Silly, really. Need never have happened. She should have been told to give up tree-climbing when she was 139.'

✳ People used to believe that if they tried hard enough, they could discover a potion which would make them live for ever. Alchemists spent all their lives mixing and stirring, trying to concoct it. They thought that liquid gold (*aurum potabile* in Latin) would do the trick.

✳ In Chichester Museum today there is a little glass bottle, which still has some pale yellow liquid in it. You can just read the label. It says *aurum potabile*. But no one has ever opened it, or knows what it really is.

✳ There was a man in the eighteenth century who called himself Count Cagliostro. He wasn't really a Count. He was a con-man. He mixed up something which he called the Elixir of Life and sold it for £1,000 per bottle. It was supposed to make you live to a hundred. Count Cagliostro died at the age of forty-nine.

The White Knight's song, by Lewis Carroll

I'll tell thee everything I can;
    There's little to relate.
I saw an aged, aged man,
    A-sitting on a gate.
'Who are you, aged man?' I said.
    'And how is it you live?'
And his answer trickled through my head,
    Like water through a sieve.

He said, 'I look for butterflies
   That sleep among the wheat:
I make them into mutton-pies,
   And sell them in the street.
I sell them unto men,' he said,
   'Who sail the stormy seas;
And that's the way I get my bread –
   A trifle, if you please.'

But I was thinking of a way
   To feed oneself on batter,
And so go on from day to day
   Getting a little fatter.
I shook him well from side to side,
   Until his face was blue.
'Come, tell me how you live,' I cried,
   'And what it is you do!'

He said, 'I hunt for haddocks' eyes
   Among the heather bright,
And work them into waistcoat buttons
   In the silent night.
And these I do not sell for gold
   Or coin of silvery shine,
But for a copper halfpenny,
   And that will purchase nine.

I sometimes dig for buttered rolls,
   Or set limed twigs for crabs;
I sometimes search the grassy knolls
   For wheels of hansom-cabs.
And that's the way,' (he gave a wink)
   'By which I get my wealth –
And very gladly will I drink
   Your Honour's noble health.'

Tea-talk

The Chinese have a legend that tea was discovered by the Emperor Shen-Hung. One day he was sitting outside in the shade of a wild tea-plant, with a pot of boiling water beside him. (Don't ask me why.) Anyway, a few leaves fell into the pot. The Emperor had a sip. 'Ouch!' he cried. That was because the water was so hot. But when it was cooler, he tried again. 'Delicious!' he cried this time. And that was how tea-drinking began.

The first cup of tea in England was drunk in Buckingham Palace in 1657. The Duke of Buckingham lived there then. It was so expensive in England that once a couple of noblemen went over to Amsterdam, bought a pound of tea there for 3s 4d, and resold it at home for £2 18s 4d. Smugglers had a good traffic in it, of course. The crypts of some churches used to be full of hidden tea. But if you weren't careful you could be diddled. The smugglers would mix it with sloes, liquorice and ash-tree leaves to make it go further.

People soon got mad about tea. The Duke of Wellington was so keen on it he made sure he had great stores of it when he went off on campaigns. And Mr Gladstone, who was one of the prime ministers during Queen Victoria's reign, used to fill his stone hot-water bottle with boiling tea, warm his feet on it first and then drink it.

But if you couldn't afford the real thing, then you could have *donkey tea* instead. You put some toast in a jug and poured some boiling water on it, left it for a while and then strained it.

✸ Tea isn't a food at all. It's a drug, which acts on the nervous system. Lots of people, like Mormons and Seventh-Day Adventists, won't drink it for that reason.

✸ Have a cup of *char*? Army people in India brought that word back with them. It comes from the Hindi word for tea, which is *cha*.

✸ There's a Leeds newsagent who drinks eighty-three cups of tea per day. (He gets up at 5.30.)

From a schoolboy essay on the Duke of Wellington: 'They gave him a lovely funeral. It took six men to carry the beer.'

Tea in Wonderland

From *Alice in Wonderland*, by Lewis Carroll

'Once upon a time, there were three little sisters,' the Dormouse began in a great hurry, 'and their names were Elsie, Lacie and Tillie; and they lived at the bottom of a well . . .'

'What did they live on?' asked Alice, who always took a great interest in questions of eating and drinking.

'They lived on treacle,' said the Dormouse, after thinking a minute or two.

'They couldn't have done that, you know,' Alice gently remarked. 'They'd have been ill.'

'So they were,' said the Dormouse; '*very* ill.'

Alice tried a little to fancy to herself what such an extraordinary way of living would be like, but it puzzled her too much, so she went on: 'But why did they live at the bottom of a well?'

'Take some more tea,' the March Hare said to Alice, very earnestly.

'I've had nothing yet,' Alice replied in an offended tone, 'so I can't take any more.'

'You mean you can't take *less*,' said the Hatter. 'It's very easy to take *more* than nothing.'

'Nobody asked *your* opinion,' said Alice.

She helped herself to some tea and bread-and-butter, and then turned to the Dormouse and repeated her question. 'Why did they live at the bottom of a well?'

The Dormouse again took a minute or two to think about it, and then said: 'It was a treacle-well.'

'There's no such thing!' Alice was beginning angrily, but the Hatter and the March Hare went 'Shh! Shh!' and the Dormouse sulkily remarked: 'If you can't be civil, you'd better finish the story for yourself.'

'No, please go on!' Alice said very humbly. 'I won't interrupt you again. I daresay there may be *one*.'

'One, indeed!' the Dormouse said indignantly. However, he consented to go on.

'And so these three little sisters – they were learning to draw, you know . . .'

'What did they draw?' said Alice, quite forgetting her promise.

'Treacle,' said the Dormouse, without considering at all, this time.

'I want a clean cup,' interrupted the Hatter. 'Let's all move one place on.'

He moved on as he spoke, and the Dormouse followed him; the March Hare moved into the Dormouse's place, and Alice rather unwillingly took the place of the March Hare. The Hatter was the only one who got any advantage from the change; and Alice was a good deal worse off than before, as the March Hare had just upset the milk jug into his plate.

Alice did not wish to offend the Dormouse again, so she began very cautiously: 'But I don't understand. Where did they draw the treacle from?'

'You can draw water out of a water-well,' said the Hatter, 'so I should think you could draw treacle out of a treacle-well – eh, stupid?'

'But they were *in* the well,' Alice said to the Dormouse, not choosing to notice this last remark.

'Of course they were,' said the Dormouse. 'Well in.'

A life on the ocean wave, with Sam Stubbins

'I'm hungry,' said Sam. He was leaning over the side of the boat doing the same thing he'd been doing for hours – not catching mackerel. 'I'd like what Rat had on his picnic with Mole – coldtonguecoldhamcoldbeefpickledgherkinssaladfrenchrollscressandwidgespottedmeatgingerbeerlemonadesodawater – only double. There's nothing nicer than unpacking things, unwrapping little packages, opening up sandwiches to see what's in them . . .' he stared dreamily out over the sea. 'What's for lunch, Minty?' he asked.

'Tuna fish sandwiches – all soft and squidgy, with lots of butter and new bread, and lettuce and mayonnaise. That's my best. And meringues, and cold chicken, and my fruit cake, and chocolate biscuits and home-made lemonade and apples and bananas . . .'

'All right,' said Sam, straightening up. 'We'll have it. Get the basket out, Steve.' (Steve was Minty's friend. It was his father's boat.)

'Where did you put it?'

'I didn't put it anywhere.'

'You must have done.'

'No, I didn't.'

They took less time not finding the basket than they had not catching mackerel.

'There were doughnuts, too,' said Bert, sadly.

'And Coke for me,' said Steve.

'And one round of cheese and chutney sandwiches just for me,' said Mrs Bert.

'And what about my pickled onions?' asked Sam.

'What about *everything*?' asked Minty.

The boat moved very gently. The sun shone. Mrs Sam, who always felt queasy as soon as she stepped on to a boat and felt it give, was – feeling queasy. She was glad about no food.

'Right,' said Sam, turning immediately into a Bold Efficient Castaway, Intrepid Explorer and All-Purpose Hero. 'It's back to the fishing rods. First person to get a fish can eat it.'

'*Raw?*' asked Steve. 'Your need is greater than mine. You can have it.'

'OK,' said Sam. 'Then we'll draw lots afterwards for which of us gets cut up first to feed the rest.'

'Sam,' said Mrs Sam faintly. 'There's a dear little fish caught on the end of my line. Could you untangle it for me? It doesn't look very happy.'

The fish was a mackerel, beautiful silver and dark sea-blue, slashed with black lines. 'You're not going to hurt it, are you?' said Mrs Sam.

Sam delved into an inside pocket of his overcoat, and brought out an orange squeezer. 'That's food and drink, that mackerel, my dear,' he said. 'What we do is – we squeeze the water out of the fish, 'cos fish is at least half made of water, then we drink the juice, mixed with a little seawater, and we stave off the deadly pangs of the demon thirst.'

'But I didn't think you could drink seawater,' said Minty. 'It's salty.'

'You only drink a tiny bit,' said Sam. 'Otherwise you just get thirstier and thirstier and full of salt till you go bonkers. Fellow called Dr Alain Bombard – he went right across the Atlantic in a little dinghy, took him sixty-seven days, and he didn't take a thing with him – on purpose. No food, no drink. Just a squeezer. Wanted to see if it could be done. And he lived on fish juice, topped up, like, with a little seawater, and fish he caught to eat, for the whole of that time. Now, where's something to catch the juice in?'

A search went on. Finally, Bert came up with a plastic thing for baling the boat with. Meanwhile, Mrs Sam was looking suspiciously pleased with herself and there was no fish.

'It wasn't happy,' she said, after Sam had ripped into her with some pretty salty nautical language. 'So I put it back. It looked very pleased.'

So that was that. Sam remembered he was an Intrepid Explorer and All-Purpose Hero, etc. 'Next thing is plankton,' he announced. 'That's good stuff. Old Bombard caught some of that with a fine net. Full of protein. Whales live on it and they do all right. Who's got a fine net?'

'But what is it?' asked Minty. 'Something like shrimps?'

'It's a mass of tiny animals,' said Sam, 'so tiny you can hardly see them. They get together in a mass, and that floats in the sea, mixed up with tiny plants. Very nourishing.'

'Sounds disgusting,' said Steve. 'Worse than raw mackerel.'

'Nourishing *and* disgusting,' said Sam. 'Lone sailors can't be choosers. There was a couple not so long ago, drifted for 188 days off the coast of South America on a little raft. Know what they ate? Fishes' eyeballs and brains. Saved their lives, too. And they drank turtles' blood.'

The trouble was, no one had a very fine net, and the water was as clear as a teardrop.

'Why don't we turn the boat round and go home?' asked Bert. This was obviously a sensible idea. But it wasn't Intrepid or Heroic or any other of the Sam things.

'Wait a sec,' said Sam. 'I bet your dad has got an emergency pack hidden somewhere, Steve. He's a good sailor. Must have one. Any idea where it could be?'

Steve had a vague idea that there *was* such a thing. 'I think it's only first-aid stuff though,' he said, 'and things like that. I remember I got sunburnt once and there was some lotion in it.'

But when they found it, it turned out to have, besides first-aid stuff, and a penknife and a compass – some vitamin tablets, glucose, a few jars of baby food, peanuts, dates and two water-bottles.

'Gosh, dates are good,' said Steve.

'And peanuts,' said Minty. 'And I'm sure baby food must be delicious.'

'You weren't so keen on it when you were a baby,' said Mrs Bert. 'You threw most of it at me.'

'Well, it's different now,' said Minty. 'This is an emergency, and besides, I'm very hungry.'

'It's a pity about the flying fish,' said Sam a little while later, leaning back and sucking a glucose tablet.

'There aren't any round here, are there?' asked Steve.

'That's the pity,' said Sam. 'Now Sir Francis Chichester – only he was just a mister then – he sailed singlehanded round the world, you know, when he was sixty-five. He had flying fish for breakfast, off the coast of Africa. They just flopped on board ready for the pan. 'Course, he had to organize himself, for a long trip like that. Took him 107 days to reach Sydney, and he was racing, too – beat the record for the trip. So he was working hard all the time. He had a little primus, to bake himself bread in. Wasn't so easy in the Roaring Forties, when the boat was tilting at thirty degrees.'

'What on earth *do* you take on a voyage like that?' asked Minty.

'Lots of fruit and nuts,' said Sam. 'He didn't eat meat, you see. Tinned sardines. Rice, flour, biscuits, butter, all that sort of thing. And mustard and cress seeds, so he had fresh green veg. Had trouble with the eggs, though. He took fourteen dozen of them, and they were important, on account of no meat. Anyway, they were coated with beeswax, to make 'em keep, but it didn't work, and they all went stinking. The pong was so bad down in his cabin, he had to toss the whole lot overboard. Actually, he started off like you, my dear,' he added, turning to Mrs Sam. 'Seasick. Went on for several days. Couldn't stand the sight of food for a while. Had to force himself to eat. You feeling all right, my dear?'

Mrs Sam wasn't feeling too good. 'I think it was that baby chicken,' she said.

'Wait a minute,' said Sam. 'I put some seasick tablets in here somewhere,' and he began turning out his pockets.

First came a packet of sandwiches – then something round, that could have been a cake. Apples and oranges filled up the cracks. That was a left-hand pocket. Out of a right one came Coke, chocolate biscuits, and something bobbly that could have been chicken. Then there were his two big inside pockets, and the one at the top . . .

'*What* have you been doing?' asked Minty, very sternly.

'Well,' said Sam. 'I remember now. I thought that hamper might get in the way, with all of us, so I emptied it out and stowed the stuff away. Best place for it, really.'

'It may be the best place,' said Minty, 'but why did you forget?'

'Well, I always keep my pockets full,' said Sam. 'It's sort of comforting. So I didn't think about it. Funny, though, I did wonder what the clinking was.'

'What about the seasick tablets?' asked Mrs Sam.

She felt so much better after one of those that she even dared to eat a meringue.

'Let's keep the fruit cake till later,' said Minty.

They sailed on for a while, so well-fed and contented that all of a sudden everything seemed easy. The sun was just right. The wind just enough, the sea all blue and green and black and strange nothing-colours. And because it didn't matter very much any more, they even caught some mackerel, seven of them.

'What a marvellous day,' said Sam, tucking into a piece of cake on the return journey. 'Here, Minty, this is a jolly good cake.'

And, although Sam was happy just to be himself again – the Sam who liked his grub – he had a vision of himself as The Lone Bold Seaman, battling his way round the Horn, buffeted by wind and waves, reefing this and letting out that, Sam Against The Sea.

'I remember,' he said out loud, 'when I was way down south of Africa and the waves were like four-storey houses leaning over me, and I had a bit of this cake – a mint cake, not a Minty cake – and I broke a tooth. Couldn't do a thing there and then, what with the waves swamping the boat, but later I got out the old dentist-kit and tried to fill it. Damn thing wouldn't hold. So I got a file and just filed it off smooth.'

'*You* did?' asked Mrs Sam.

'Did I say me?' said Sam, coming out of his daydream. 'I meant Sir Francis.'

And he fell back into that other world again – saw himself sailing into Plymouth with little boats fluttering all round his battered *Gipsy Moth* – saw himself at Greenwich, kneeling before the Queen, and Sir Francis Drake's own sword tapped his shoulder – 'Arise, Sir Sam.'

Sam turned and looked at the little port as it grew and grew in front of him. Home. Land. Solid land.

'Well,' said Sam. 'See you next week, then? Make us another lunch like that then, will you, Minty, there's a good girl?'

'All right,' said Minty. 'I'll make it. And I'll be in charge of it, too. Off *and* on the boat. Thanks for a lovely day, anyway. And that overcoat of yours isn't the right thing for sailing in, really. You ought to get a proper anorak, or something. I bet Sir Francis had one. With smaller pockets, though, so you don't get ideas.'

Minty's fruit cake

What you need
200 gr ($\frac{1}{2}$ lb) of self-raising flour
100 gr ($\frac{1}{4}$ lb) of sugar
300 gr ($\frac{3}{4}$ lb) of mixed dried fruit
2 eggs
100 gr ($\frac{1}{4}$ lb) of butter, melted but not oily
$\frac{1}{4}$ teaspoon of mixed spice
$\frac{1}{4}$ teaspoon of ground nutmeg
1 teacupful of milk
pinch of salt
few drops of vanilla
1 cake tin, a wooden spoon or electric beater
a large mixing bowl, a cake rack

How to make it

1 Turn the oven to 325° F, gas No 3.

2 Grease the cake tin.

3 Put all the ingredients into the large mixing bowl.

4 Beat everything together for 5 minutes with the wooden spoon, or for just a couple of minutes with the electric beater.

5 Spoon the mixture into the cake tin, and make the top smooth.

6 Put into the bottom of the oven and bake for 2 hours.

7 Let the cake cool for a while. Ease the sides away from the cake tin all the way down, with a knife. Put the cake rack (or the rack from the grill if you haven't got one) on top of the cake, and turn the whole thing upside-down. Leave the cake to get cold.

There isn't an easier cake to make, and it tastes delicious. If you eat it very soon after cooking, it will be rather crumbly and hard to cut, but if you leave it for several hours, it will be much firmer.

Fisherman's toast

What you need

3 eggs

2 tablespoonsful of milk

salt and pepper

oil for frying

several thin slices of bread

How to make it

1 Beat the eggs and milk together in the bowl, and add salt and pepper.

2 Cut each slice of bread into 3 fingers.

3 Put the frying pan on to the hotplate (or gas-ring), and put in enough oil to cover the bottom to a depth of about 10 mm ($\frac{1}{2}''$). Heat the oil. (But don't keep the gas or electricity too high, once the fat is really hot, or you will burn the bread.)

4 Dip the fingers of bread in the egg mixture. Take them out again with a large spoon, and put them *gently* into the hot oil, so as the oil won't splash and burn you.

5 Fry the pieces of bread for just a minute or two, watching carefully to see when they go brown.

6 Take them out. Keep them warm, until you have used up all the egg mixture with the next lot of fingers.

7 Turn the heat off.

These are delicious with tomato ketchup, or to go with a piece of cheese. They make a good quick supper. Fishermen in Wales eat them after a fishing trip.

Poor knights

These are a bit like fisherman's toast, but not so eggy, and you eat them with jam, as a pudding. Use one less egg, and cream instead of milk, if you have it. Fry the bread as before, and dust it with sugar and a little cinnamon.

Nutty nosh

It's easy to live with the gerbil,
His diet's exclusively herbal.
    He just munches and crunches
    Long vegetable lunches,
And charms every ear with his burble.

There was an old fellow of Malta,
Who strangled his aunt with a halter.
    He said, 'I won't bury her,
    She'll do for my terrier,
She'll keep for a month if I salt her.'

There was a young lady of Ryde,
Who ate a green apple and died.
  The apple fermented
  Inside the lamented,
And made cider inside her inside.

Hard living

If you're ever stuck in the wilds and have to live off the land, here are some wild things you could eat. (**Important** Before eating anything growing, make absolutely sure it is what you think it is! There are a lot of plants and berries that wouldn't do you any good at all.)

Nettles can be cooked like cabbage, and make quite good soup. (I've eaten it.) The old leaves can be a bit leathery, but they certainly don't sting.

Sorrel is delicious too, for soups.

Dandelions are a very good vegetable, full of vitamins A and C. You can eat the leaves raw in salads, or cook them. Some Red Indian tribes used to make tea out of their roots.

Cow parsnip is a big white flower that grows in hedges. You can eat the leaves and the flower stalks.

Bracken was once a very important Red Indian food. When the stalks grow tall, they get very tough and slightly poisonous. But when they are no more than about 20 cm (8″) high, they can be boiled in salted water for three-quarters of an hour, and eaten with salt, pepper and melted butter. They are *supposed* to taste like asparagus. I tried them once, and they were just eatable. Better than nothing, if you're really hungry.

Clover leaves are good when they're small.

Hawthorn shoots and the new small leaves taste nice raw.

Fireweed is a tall weed, with purple flowers all up it, that grows wild on wasteland, in the town as well as the country. You can eat the young shoots, and use the flower stalks and leaves in salads.

The trouble with vegetable food is that it isn't very filling, and there's not much protein in it. So to keep really fit, you'd have to try and catch a rabbit or two, or poach fish, or even kill some birds. But one of the best wild things is **nuts**.

Chestnuts – the Spanish kind. The Red Indians used to crush them, and skim off the oil. (All nuts are full of oil.)

Beechnuts are good and nourishing. So are most *pine-nuts*. (The Italians use them a lot in cooking.)

The *inner bark* of all *pine-trees* is edible.

Acorns – you can eat these, but they are very bitter. If you can get rid of the bitterness, then you can grind them into flour and make bread. If you want to make acorn bread, like the Indians of Round Valley in America, this is what you have to do. First, dry the nuts in the sun, then grind them into a fine flour with a stone mortar (this is hard work). Then put them into a hollow of earth or stones, and let water run through them for a couple of hours. This is essential, to remove the bitterness. The acorn meal is then wet and soggy, like dough. The Indians mix it with red clay, one portion of clay to twenty of dough. This makes the bread sweet – some say it works like yeast and helps the bread to rise.

The next thing is to make a small fire on some stones, to heat them. Then put a bed of oak twigs on the rocks, and put the dough on it. Cover with leaves and a layer of hot rocks and mud, to keep the heat in. Leave to cook gently for twelve hours. Next morning (if you've left it all night) you'll have a black-looking loaf, which isn't soft like our bread, but more like hard cheese! In a few days it will become hard and black like coal. But you could still eat it, if you were desperate.

✳ Ground and roasted acorns are used to make a kind of coffee (the acorns being well soaked first).

Horse-chestnuts can be used in an emergency – but they are **poisonous** unless you soak them for several days to remove the deadly aesculin which is in them.

Apart from plants and nuts, there are also fruits and other growing things you could eat . . .

Blackberries – of course.

Elderberries are small and black, and hang in bunches on the elder tree. You can make wine out of them, besides eating them. The flowers are white and are good in pancakes.

Sloes are dark purple and very bitter. Some people use them to flavour drinks.

Seaweed used to be eaten a lot by the Indians on the Pacific coast of America. Especially the kinds called *kelp* and *laver*, which are full of iodine. The Welsh make something called laver bread.

Carageen moss is a pale yellowy colour. You cook it rather like rice pudding, so that it goes solid and spongy. It's meant to be very good for you.

Mushrooms are good, too, but getting scarcer in the wild. It's safer not to try any toadstools unless you really know about them, except for –

Puffballs, which are unmistakable. They are white, and as round as a ball. When you tread on them, they explode into white smoke. The Iroquoi fry them and add them to soups. The Omaha cut the large ones into chunks and fry them like meat. And the Blackfoot Indians use the inside of dried, unripe puffballs to stop wounds bleeding.

✳ The Menominee tribe of Indians used to live in a place where lots of wild leeks grew. The leeks smelt so strong that the Indians named the place 'skika'ko', which means 'skunk-place'. This place is now called Chicago.

What's the first message a Red Indian sent as a smoke signal? 'Help, my blanket's on fire!'

Some people in South America and Africa take lumps of earth, mostly the clay or chalk kind, make them into little pancakes and grill them over a hot fire. Sometimes they mix up marshy clay with fruit juices and make a kind of jam.

The Quecha Indians, who live high up in the Andes mountains of Peru, have very little food to eat. But they are very healthy. Experts couldn't understand why – until they discovered that the Indians used clay to make a sauce for their potatoes. And they put powdered rock ash in their porridge. This way, they eat valuable minerals, like calcium.

The strange story of the bacon tree

One day, a German General and a few of his soldiers found themselves absolutely alone, lost and hungry in the middle of the hot burning desert of North Africa. For days they had struggled on, but every day they were no nearer civilization.

'Vere can ve be, Klaus?' the General asked his young lieutenant one day.

'I do not know, Herr General. But if ve do not find some food or drink soon, ve vill die. Vot shall ve do?'

'You must go avay und look, Klaus. Ve vill stay here und vait for you. Gott in Himmel, I cannot stand der heat.'

And the General sat down, and poor old Klaus set off into the desert. The sun climbed higher and higher into the sky. The sand shimmered and the air above it trembled with heat. Klaus staggered on, almost fainting from lack of water, over miles of sand dunes. There wasn't a tree. There wasn't any living thing. And then – suddenly he saw it! There, in the distance, there *was* a tree. He saw it clearly. It wasn't very tall, but it had wide branches, and hanging from every branch he saw rashers of bacon, sizzling in the sun. He could swear he could almost smell it. A bacon tree!

Klaus turned back. What a find! Food at last, just for the taking. He had to get back to the others quickly and tell them about it. So he

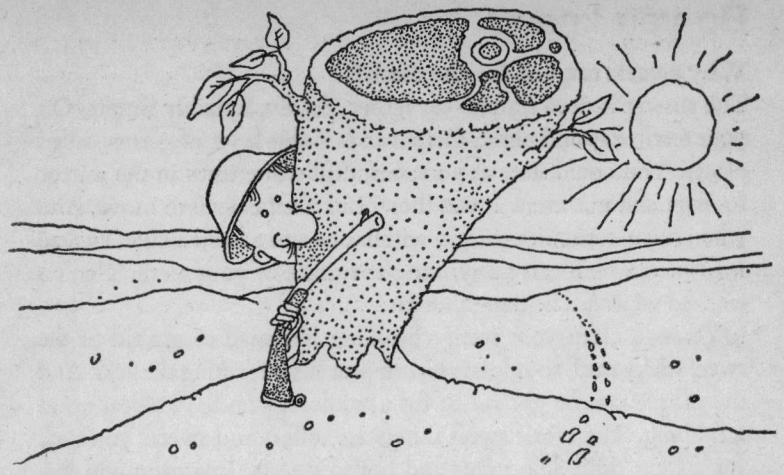

trudged on until at last he found his comrades, just where he'd left them.

'Vell?' asked the General. 'Vot did you see?'

'A bacon tree, Herr General.'

'A *bacon tree*?'

'Ja, Herr General. Hurry, follow me. Zair iss food out zair. Und no time to lose. Der heat iss getting vorse.'

So the General and the rest of his small group of soldiers wearily got to their feet, and followed Klaus. It was a terrible journey, for the sun was by now at its zenith. Finally, as they were just staggering over the top of a sand dune, Klaus shouted: 'Zair iss der tree!' Pointing ahead, he began to run towards it.

At that moment, the enemy suddenly rushed out at them from behind another sand dune, and wiped out the lot of them, except for the General and Klaus, who was wounded. The General came over to Klaus, who was lying in the sand, bent down and spoke to him. 'Klaus, you said it vos a bacon tree. You vere wrong, my friend. Zat vos no bacon tree – zat vos a ham bush.'

Do you know?

Why sweets are bad for the teeth?

The answer is dead simple – or rather, deadly, horribly simple. On your teeth, day and night, there is an invisible layer of germs, called *plaque*. You could stare at your beautiful white teeth in the mirror for ever and not know it was there. But it's the devil to move. And when sugar combines with it, within one and a half minutes an acid is formed which eats away into the surface of your teeth. That's a fact. So what can be done about it?

You can clean your teeth – brushing like mad to get rid of the sweet sticky stuff, so at least you can prevent it forming the acid. And the plaque can be got rid of for a while, if you have a real go at scrubbing. The worst sweet things are toffees and sweets you suck for a long time, like mints and boiled sweets. Ice-cream and ice-lollies, too, stay around in the mouth for longer than you'd think.

Every year, British children lose a total of four million teeth. And I don't mean they just fall out – they're hoiked out, by the dentist.

What our oldest national dish is?

It's probably something called 'frumenty'. We know it was eaten in England in the Iron Age. It's made with whole fresh wheat which is soaked (they call it 'creeing the wheat'), and then left in a cool oven for a day. The grains swell and turn into a jelly, a bit like frog-spawn. Then you can add milk and eggs, or spice and raisins, sugar or rum. (In the book *The Mayor of Casterbridge*, by Thomas Hardy, it was on sale at Weyhill Fair, laced with rum.)

What a red herring is?

A red herring is a herring that has been dried, smoked and salted. Poor people ate them a lot in the old days, before refrigeration. It was cheaper than meat, and the poor didn't have their own fish-ponds, like the rich people and the monks. So when people say something is 'Neither fish, flesh, nor good red herring', they mean it's not any good for anyone at all.

If a red herring is drawn across a fox's path, it destroys the scent and puts the hounds off. So a 'red herring' in a detective story means something that puts you off the track, like a false clue.

What a 'peppercorn rent' is?

Nowadays, if you let a house for a 'peppercorn rent', it means you rent it for very little. But in the thirteenth century, people really did rent land and property for a payment of peppercorns. Usually it was a pound of pepper a year. And it meant a fair amount, because pepper might cost anything between 10d and 2s 4d a pound – and an unskilled worker was paid only 2d a day.

✳ In 1383 you could buy a goose for 6d – and three roast pigeons for 2½d.

✳ People used to brown the outside of their meat, and sprinkle gunpowder on it instead of salt.

Two-time one piecey swim-swim

(or: Sam and Bert have a meal of fish and chips)

'These are good,' said Bert, licking his fingers.

'Hmm,' said Sam. 'Too much batter and not enough fish.'

'Oh, the batter's the best bit,' said Bert. 'All crisp and crunchy.

Wonder how they make it?'

'Well,' replied Sam, 'they've tried all sorts of things – Guinness, eggs, lemon, mixed up with it. But your real expert just uses flour, water and a spot of bicarbonate of soda. Then he leaves it a bit – and Bob's your uncle.'

'The chips are great,' went on Bert, munching away. 'Soft inside and a bit crackly outside. Yum. Just how I like 'em. I could go on eating 'em for ever. Chips . . .' he said, holding one up and turning it round, 'what a great British invention.'

'British invention nothing,' retorted Sam, as they walked on. 'Wrong and double wrong, matey. Now, *battered* fish, that's different. That *was* a British invention. Know what happened when there was a fight in a fish and chip shop, by the way?'

'Four fish got battered.'

'Right. Well, your Englishman was always a great fish-batterer. Back in the 1860s you'd get a bloke shouting round the pubs, "Fish and bread a penny!" Think of it – a lovely hot piece of fried fish in batter *and* a hunk of bread, all for an old penny . . .'

'But what about the chips?' asked Bert.

'Well, there was a Mr Lees, up in Lancashire. Sold fish. Now, one day, he heard of a fellow who was selling "chipped potatoes in the French style", so he put one and one together and made fish and chips.'

'So that's when it started, then?'

'Could be. But there's a shop in London, called Malin's – they say that *they're* the oldest fish and chip shop in the world. They started in 1865.'

'Well, I bet we're the only country to have 'em, anyway,' said Bert. 'Got any more chips, by the way?'

Sam just happened to have a spare packet in the top right-hand pocket of his overcoat.

'Wrong and treble wrong,' he said. 'You can get them all over the place. They're catching, you know. You get an Englishman in a foreign country – he says, "Where's the fish and chips, then?" – so someone starts cooking. You can find 'em in Germany and Belgium and Holland, and down in Spain where the tourists go. All the Commonwealth countries, too, like Australia and Canada. And if you go way down to Suva in Fiji, there's a Chinese shop selling the stuff there, even.'

Bert munched on, thoughtfully. 'Well, it's a great British export, anyway.'

Sam finished the last of his, and stuffed the paper in his pocket. 'Ever heard of a place called Abu Dhabi?'

Bert shook his head.

'It's in the Middle East,' said Sam, 'where the sand is. Now, I'll tell you a good café to go to there. Called the Al-Samakeh Al Thahabiya café.'

'Thanks,' said Bert.

'That's the Golden Fish Snack Bar. Opened a couple of years ago. 'Course, it's not cod and chips there, it's *hammour* and chips, but you'd never guess, inside all that batter.'

'OK,' said Bert. 'I'll pop in, next time I'm buying an oil well . . . Oh blimey, I was supposed to buy some fish and chips for the wife . . .'

'Well, as it happens,' said Sam, burrowing in his bottom left-hand pocket . . . 'Here you are, one piecey swim-swim, now you fly him, now potatoes,' and he handed Bert a hot newspaper parcel.

'Sounds like a bikini,' said Bert. 'What on earth is it?'

'It's pidgin English for fish and chips,' said Sam. 'That's what you order when you're down in Singapore. One piecey swim-swim – that's the fish. If you want *two* portions, then it's *two-time* one piecey swim-swim. Then you fry him, but they're not too good at saying "r", so they say fly instead. And then you've got potatoes, that's the chips. It's simple, really.'

'Fish and chips is simplest,' said Bert. 'I'll stick to *that*.'

✳ The biggest fish and chip shop in the world is called Harry Ramsden's, and it's in Guiseley, in Yorkshire. One Easter Monday, they served 2,500 customers in the restaurant, and some 4,000 in the take-away shop.

✳ 40% of all the white fish sold in Britain goes into fish and chips. Every year, 600,000 tons of potatoes turn into chips, and 80,000 tons of oil and fat go to frying them.

✳ A man called Haddon Salt opened a fish and chip shop in California. The food was wrapped in printed replicas of the front page of *The Times*.

✳ There's a chain of fish and chip shops in America, including: 'Hungry Penguin Fish and Chips', 'Ye Fish Chips'n Ale', and 'HMS Cod'.

✳ Fish and chips contain: proteins, carbohydrates, fats, fluoride, calcium, iodine, nicotinic acid and vitamins A, B1 and B2, C and D.

A frier (whose name doesn't matter)
Went suddenly mad as a hatter.
He went for his knife,
And cut up his wife,
And sold her as scampi in batter.

Food quiz 4
Call my bluff

Here are three definitions for each word. One is correct, the other two are not. Which is the right definition? (Answers on page 154.)

Cous-cous

1 Cous-cous are millet flour dumplings, boiled in water and served with mutton, usually. An Arabian dish.

2 Cous-cous are a very sweet biscuit, made mostly of honey, which the Turks eat with very strong black coffee.

3 Cous-cous is a South American fruit, rather like a small tomato, with lots of pips in it. It is sometimes made into an alcoholic drink.

Mishmish

1 Mishmish is a kind of Middle Eastern apricot.

2 Mishmish is a kind of sausage the Moroccans make out of camel flesh.

3 Mishmish is a Siamese dish of boiled rice and vegetables.

Camu-camu

1 Camu-camu is a Mexican dish made of soya beans, and is very nourishing and full of protein.

2 Camu-camu is a favourite drink of the Tibetans, made of rancid butter, and is thought to be one of the most healthy foods in the world.

3 Camu-camu is a fruit which grows in the Amazon Basin, which has forty-five times more vitamin C in it than an orange.

Pawpaw

1 The pawpaw is the fruit of a South American tree. The juice from the stalk is used to tenderize meat.

2 The pawpaw is a tuber, like a potato, which grows in Central America. The leaves are used for making hats.

3 The pawpaw is the pidgin English name which Indonesian people have given to a pig's trotter. They hang them up in their houses to keep devils away.

Odd man out

1 You can eat everything in the following list except one. Which one?

broccoli, botticelli, vermicelli, tagliatelle, ravioli

2 All these words are names of different cheeses, except one. Which one?

gorgonzola, gruyère, Giorgione, gouda, Gloucester

3 All these names are connected with food in some way, except one. Which one?

Charlotte, Johnny, Véronique, Melba, Anne, Baba, Rosemary

4 Which word is *not* something that a cook does to food?

braise, banter, baste, broil, bake, blanch, boil

5 Which of these is *not* a herb used in cooking?

thyme, mint, parsley, tarragon, teazle, fennel, savory, marjoram

6 One of these words has nothing at all to do with cooking or food. Which one?

fritter, flummery, flutter, frumenty, flounder, fricassée

(Answers on page 154)

Mad medicines

In the seventeenth century they diagnosed some crazy diseases, like:

Glimming of the Gizzard

The Wambling Trot

The Moon-Pall

The Martambles

Quavering of the kidneys

The Strong Fives

The Hockogrockle

Whirligigousticon (actually malaria)

Obviously, if you've got a desperate disease like one of those, then you need a desperate cure, such as . . .

Mummies Pulverized mummies were a very powerful medicine. After all, a mummy had lasted a long, long time, so it ought to do the same thing for the patient. The mummy of a criminal who had been hanged was specially good.

Spiders rolled in butter. A daily dose of a clean spider's web was just the thing for curing fevers.

The Black Powder This cured the most dreaded disease of all – smallpox. It was a powder made of thirty to forty burnt toads.

Swallows Eating swallows was good for the sight, according to a Book of Knowledge in 1687.

A hangman's rope Soak the rope used to hang a man, and drink the water. That's a cure for a bad headache.

✴ The best cure of all, though, was the Gold Cure – something called *aurum potabile*, or liquid gold, because they believed gold was the most 'perfect' substance and was bound to produce perfect health.

✴ And all pills are to be taken only in *odd numbers*.

Crazy cures, eighteenth-century style

For measles Get someone to put a live sheep on the end of your bed. This will cure you, because sheep are very easily infected, and will take the measles out of you, and into them. (No one mentions, as far as I know, how you keep the sheep on the bed, or how you cure a sheep of the measles.)

For toothache Carry a dead person's tooth in your pocket. This is a certain cure (so they say). Alternatively, take some worms and put them on a hot stone to dry. When they crumble to powder, stuff it in the hollow of your tooth. This will make sure the tooth falls out – and the toothache with it.

For a sty A sty used to be called a 'stiony' – sty-on-eye. The cure for this is easy. Rub it with the tail of a black cat.

To prevent nightmares Anoint the soles of your feet with the fat of a dormouse. Anoint your teeth with the earwax of a dog, swine's gall and hare's ears.

For hiccups Spit on your right forefinger. Cross the front of your left shoe with it three times, repeating the Lord's Prayer backwards.

✳ The world's worst hiccuppers

In the summer of 1974, there was a report in English newpapers about a West German called Heinz Isecke. He had been hiccupping continuously forty times a minute for eight months, and was 'weakening dangerously'. Even at night he would be woken up by the hiccups every few minutes. And even a special operation on his vagus nerve didn't cure it. What was he to do?

He was sent two thousand anti-hiccup tips from all over the world. British people suggested seaweed tablets, opium, iodine and sugar, a tablespoon of English mustard, and drinking out of the wrong side of a cup, among others. But within a week of publicizing his predicament he was cured – by another German, a chemist, who sent him an extract of twelve different herbal oils and chlorophyl. He took the first tablespoonful on a Sunday morning, and by the evening the hiccups had stopped!

The world's very worst case was Jack O'Leary of Los Angeles. He hiccupped 160 million times between 1948 and 1956. He tried sixty thousand remedies. Finally, he sent up a prayer to St Jude (the patron saint of lost causes), and was cured.

(For ordinary everyday hiccups this has always worked for me: just eat a heaped teaspoon of granulated sugar.)

Old cough mixtures

For an ordinary cough

1 Take two or three snails and boil them in barley water. Dose yourself several times with the mixture.

2 Take an old owl, and two puppies. Stew them. Eat them.

For whooping cough

1 Get three fieldmice. Take the innards out of them, and then roast one and eat it. Dry the other two in the oven until they crumble into powder. Put a little of this powder in your drink night and morning.

2 (You need some outside help with this one.) The patient is drawn, naked, nine times over the back and under the belly of a three-year-old donkey. Take three spoonsful of the donkey's milk, and put three hairs from the donkey's back, and three hairs from its belly, into the milk; let it stand for three hours. Give the patient three doses of this mixture.

3 Get a hairy caterpillar and put it in a small bag. Tie the bag around your neck. As the caterpillar dies, your cough will disappear.

The pebble cure

This is supposed to be a true story, but it happened a long time ago . . .

There was once a man called Thomas Gobsill, who suffered terribly from wind. When he was twenty-six, and fed up with burping and belching all the time, he took a friend's advice. Take nine pebbles a day, the friend said, and all your troubles will be over.

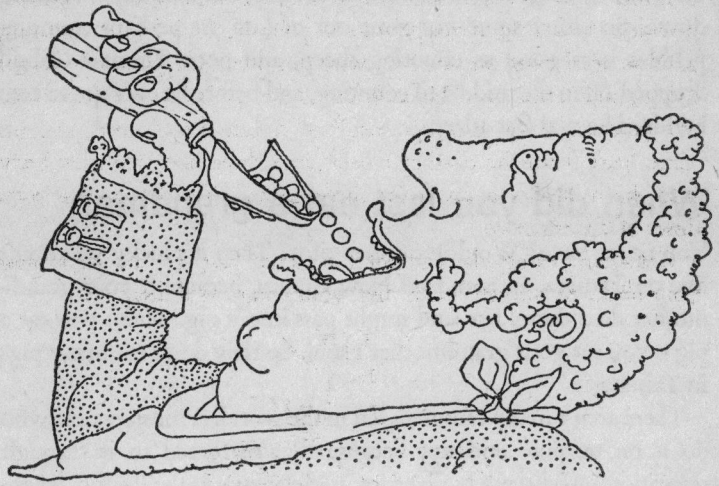

Gobsill did as he was told. He swallowed the pebbles, and hey presto, he seemed to be cured. The wind disappeared, the pebbles came out the other end, and everything was fine. But then his trouble came back, and worse than before. He was in agony. So this time he increased the dose. And he increased it so much that in the end he swallowed *two hundred* pebbles (only little ones, though).

So now he suffered from pebbles. It was worse than wind. His stomach was loaded, and they didn't come out of the other end any more. So a famous physician called Sir Charles Hall came to the rescue. He came to Gobsill's house, and called for a ladder. They put it against the wall. And the house was on the village green, so naturally a great crowd of people gathered to see what was happening. While they watched, Sir Charles upended Gobsill, strapped him to the ladder head-down, and then gave the ladder an almighty shake. The stones rattled down, but they didn't come out. And when Gobsill was turned the right way up again, everyone heard the two hundred pebbles settling in place again.

Poor Gobsill. He just had to live with them. No one knows what happened to him in the end, but we do know he had trouble lying down. For the pebbles wouldn't stay down in his stomach, and he'd have to get up on his knees until they dropped back down again. Now the story goes that he used to count about a hundred clinking down. So either some *had* gone out of him, or perhaps counting pebbles is as good as counting sheep, and poor Thomas Gobsill dropped off in the middle of counting, and before he ever got to two hundred he was fast asleep.

When did you last eat a grandma?

You never have? Wouldn't dream of it? Then it's lucky you don't live on Tamara, an island off New Guinea, because if your grandmother died there, her soul might pass into a pig. Then, you eat a pig – you eat your grandmother's soul. So they don't eat many pigs in Tamara.

There aren't many cannibals left in the world. (I mean people who do it on purpose and not because they're forced to it through starvation.) There used to be a lot in Melanesia, in the Pacific, where they called human meat 'long pig', and in Polynesia. They say it still goes on in New Guinea, and the Batak of Sumatra are cannibals.

Human flesh tastes quite good, so they say. Especially the upper parts of the arm. But that wasn't the reason people ate it. Sometimes it was part of a magic ritual. Or murderers would eat their victims so the ghosts wouldn't come back and haunt them. But in some parts of Africa, people would find themselves in the stewpot because they were extra good, or brave. The Africans would eat their vital parts, like hearts and livers, to get that goodness or bravery for themselves. It's strange – but probably many missionaries were eaten, not because they were hated, but because they were admired! (Dr Livingstone's heart mysteriously disappeared from his body after he died.)

The most recent well-known case of cannibalism happened in 1972. An aeroplane crashed high up in the Andes, with forty-five people on board, most of them young Uruguayan rugby players. Searchers failed to find them. They were given up as lost. And then, seventy-two days later, they were found. Some of them. Sixteen of them were still alive. But they weren't haggard scarecrows, they were hale and hearty. How could that be, asked everyone. It was because they ate the people who died in the crash. They all felt a deep revulsion against it, but in the end, a few managed to stomach the idea. They cut off strips of meat and hung them up to dry. (Some couldn't face the prospect. And they died of starvation.)

Food taboos

Eating people is *wrong*. Most people believe that. It is taboo. That means it is forbidden by custom, habit or religion. It's a very peculiar thing, why some people eat this, but won't eat that. Take something quite ordinary to us, like bacon and eggs . . .

How about bacon and eggs?

'Not for me, thanks,' says a vegetarian.

'No, thank you,' says a Jew. 'Bacon is disgusting. I wouldn't touch it.'

'An *egg*?' says a Yaka woman from the Congo. 'If I touched one of those, I'd go mad, rip off my clothes and run away into the bush.'

'A *fresh* egg?' says a man from the Philippines. 'Certainly not. I only eat eggs which a hen has sat on for at least ten days, with the chickens beginning to grow.'

'Eggs?' says a Brahmin. 'I don't want to see them. Last time I even saw one being broken I was violently ill.'

'Bacon? From a *pig*?' says a Moslem. 'That's strictly forbidden.'

So many different reasons. But mostly religious, or some deep-held tribal belief or fear. Now maybe, before the religions fixed these taboos, there was another reason. In the very old days, people were either shepherds, looking after flocks of sheep and cattle, or they were cultivaters, going after wild pigs and suchlike. And each group of people despised the other. And to show it, they wouldn't touch any food that the other lot ate. And so there grew up a hatred of pigs, say, in some people, and a hatred of beef and mutton in others. And different religions fixed that hatred for ever – saying: Pigs are unclean, you mustn't touch them. Or, It's wicked to eat beef . . .

Now, the Buddhists believe you shouldn't harm *any* living thing – so they won't kill animals for food. Many vegetarians believe this too. There was a very great Indian leader some years ago called Gandhi, who belonged to a group of Hindus who wouldn't eat meat or fish. But he thought perhaps he ought to *try* it once. So he ate some goat's meat. He found it as tough as leather. And afterwards he had a terrible nightmare. 'Every time I dropped off to sleep,' he said, 'it would seem as though a live goat were bleating inside me.' So he never touched meat again.

Now, some people wouldn't eat frogs or snails, or jellied eels, or tripe, or semolina or spinach. But if you believe that something is really taboo, then you'd actually *die* rather than eat it.

The Jains in India believe that *everything* has life, not just animals. Plants, air, water, clay. And to take life is a sin. So, when they walk along the road, they sweep the ground in front of them, in case they tread on an ant, or some small creature. They veil their mouths, to protect the air from their breath. And they never eat after dark in case they accidentally destroy some insect. They won't eat anything fermented, like cheese or yoghurt, or root vegetables, like carrots. They *will* eat fruit, if it falls from a tree.

The Nambikwara Indians of Brazil keep lots of animals, like chickens. But they keep them as pets, playing with them, and talking to them. They don't even eat the eggs their hens lay. Julius Caesar, by the way, reported that the Britons in his time wouldn't eat chickens. They only kept them because they liked them.

✳ Lobsters are cannibals.

✳ The Ojibwa Indians in North America would sometimes get a sudden desperate urge to eat human flesh. They dreaded this feeling, but couldn't do anything about it. It was put into them by the fearsome Windigo, who was a cannibal giant and lived deep in the woods.

✱ And talking of bacon and eggs for breakfast ... On the side of a French packet of cornflakes, you can find a description of a 'very English breakfast', as follows. 'Place two fried eggs (not overdone) in a plateful of cornflakes. Season with salt and pepper and eat without delay.'

But eat up – this food will do you good!

The Abipones of Paraguay eat *jaguars*, *bulls* and *stags* to make themselves swift, strong and brave.

The Miris of Assam are very keen on *tiger's* flesh to make themselves fierce. But their women are definitely not allowed to touch it.

Kansas Indians like *dog's* flesh, because it will make them brave and faithful.

The Malays of Singapore eat *tiger* too, and the Hottentots eat *lion*, to get the strength and courage of those animals.

Some American Indians believe that a person who eats venison (*deer*) is much swifter and wiser than people who eat clumsy *bears*, or stupid *hens*, or slow-footed *cows*, or wallowing *pigs*.

There once was a very old gnu,
Who was used by a chief in some stew.
He should have been told
The gnu was too old:
For stews, only new gnus will do.

But the Dyaks of Borneo won't eat *deer* in case they get that animal's timidity. And both the Caribs and Zulu girls won't eat *pigs* in case their eyes become small and they begin to look like pigs themselves.

One day, a gorilla went into a pub, and ordered a pint of beer. He handed over a pound note, and the publican, being a greedy man, handed him just one penny change, and said, 'We don't get many gorillas in here.' Replied the gorilla, 'I'm not surprised, considering the prices you charge.'

Insect grub

Grasshoppers are best stuffed. The Chinese and Japanese grill or fry them, cover them in sauce and wrap them in pancakes.

Locusts are very good to eat – there's more protein in locusts than there is in beef. John the Baptist, remember, lived entirely for a while on locusts and wild honey.

Worms – the Mexicans get really big, fat wriggly ones from palm trees. They oil and fry them, roll them in sugar, and sell them on street corners as we sell chestnuts.

Some pygmy tribes leave their carcasses of meat especially to go rotten, and *then* eat them. This way, they get the meat, plus all the goodness of health-giving worms as well.

Butterflies are supposed to make a delicious crunchy food. The Kapapalo Indians take the wings off, cook them and chew them. The Ethiopians eat their own brand of enormous winged insects – roasted.

Termites are a kind of ant. They are a great delicacy in India. You'd have to go to Africa to eat a *termite sausage*.

Lizards Apparently, Australian Aborigine children are very fond of a giant lizard called a 'dob'. These are grilled. Then you slit the skin down the middle and pick out the cooked bits inside.

Maggots and the pupa of the wasp are very rich in vitamin A.

Witchetty grubs are the larvae of the longicorn beetle. They are four or five inches long and as thick as your finger. The people in New

Guinea dig them out of the roots of eucalyptus trees and eat them lightly roasted.

Beetles The Japanese take off the hard shell, fry the bodies and mix them with sugar.

Water-beetles may be very important food in the future, for astronauts. They are very easy to rear, cook and eat, and they are packed with nourishment. It's being said now that when astronauts go on really long voyages, they'll breed water-beetles, to eat as they go along.

The case of the supermarket cockroach

This is a true story. Some people in America brought a court case against a supermarket. They said there were cockroaches running about there, and getting in the food, and this was unhygienic and disgusting. They lost their case. This was after the defence lawyer stood up in court and publicly ate a cockroach – raw.

Far-out food in the Far East

What's on the menu in Peking?

Puppy hams The Chinese have been eating dogs for centuries. They bred the Chow specially for eating. (Chairman Mao, though, has been having a blitz on Chinese dogs, because there are so many around.)

Camel paw and camel hump – if they're in season.

Sea slug Some people call this a sea cucumber. It's a simple jellyish animal that lives at the bottom of the sea. It's very slippery.

Sweet and sour pork In 1957, China had a quarter of all the pigs in the world, fourteen million. They are useful animals, as they eat up scraps and leftovers. Most people in China today can't afford to eat it, though. Sweet and sour sauce goes on lots of Chinese food – it's basically vinegar and sugar.

Bird's nest soup is only made from one kind of nest, which is made by a bird like a martin, which sticks its nest to walls and caves. The sticky stuff the bird makes is almost colourless, so the soup is rather pale and gelatinous.

Hundred-year-old-eggs? They aren't really. What the Chinese do is bake the egg very slowly in a coating of clay and lime for *two weeks* so that the white turns brownish and the yolk goes dark purple.

✳ **News item** 18 December, Tokyo. A restaurant for dogs opened in Tokyo today. Rows of tiny tables and chairs are set in the dining room with a brightly decorated Christmas tree.

✳ The Chinese word for 'home' is made up of the sign for 'roof' and 'pig'.

✳ A big treat for people in Annam, in South-East Asia, would be a dog-chop and a cup of rice wine.

Food quiz 5
What are they?

All these are either kinds of food, or something to do with cooking.

1 mangelwurzel
2 horseradish
3 samovar
4 sweetbreads
5 shish-kebab
6 kedgeree
7 arrowroot
8 skillet
9 dill
10 yeast
11 roll-mop
12 rissole
13 soufflé
14 colander
15 guava
16 kipper

(Answers on page 155)

True or false?

1 Carrots make you see in the dark.
2 Fish make you brainy.
3 You could live on milk alone.
4 Spinach makes you strong.
5 You can only eat oysters when there's an R in the month.
6 Green potatoes are poisonous.
7 Swallowing pips gives you appendicitis.
8 You shouldn't eat mushrooms and almond icing at the same meal.
9 Raw vegetables are better for you than cooked ones.
10 Cabbage cleans the blood, and makes your hair curl.

(Answers on page 155)

```
GRISSLEGREESE GRAMMAR SCHOOL

          PIG SWILL MENU
    Everything guaranteed YMCA
    Yesterday's Muck Cooked Again



             FIRST COURSE
   Choice of three very slightly warm dishes

            Special Irish spew
swimming in bilge and enriched with added gristle
         With garbage and door steps

                   or

             Resurrection Pie
      Served with overcooked seaweed
        and undercooked cannonballs

                   or

              Armoured Cow
   Served with worms and rabbit's food



             SECOND COURSE

      Frog's spawn or snottie gog pie

                   or

            Stodge in Brylcreem


  (If your helping is too small, please help yourself
              to a magnifying glass)
```

(For a translation, see page 156)

The case of the wicked lollipop and the disappearing puddings

Minty found Sam Stubbins lolling in a deckchair in his back garden. He was having tea. She threw her satchel down, and grabbed a biscuit.

'I'm famished,' she said.

'Had a good lunch at school, today?' asked Sam.

'Smashing. Gristle stew. One potato. I couldn't eat the second course. It was a new kind of frog's spawn and jam with lots of wooden pips. Steve ate mine. He had seconds, too.'

'Lucky fellow,' said Sam.

'Needs his head examining,' said Minty. 'Can I have another biscuit, do you think?'

'Wait a minute,' said Sam. 'I think I've got something special.' He leant over and grubbed up something that looked like an onion from the flowerbed behind him.

'But that's a bulb,' said Minty. 'You don't eat those.'

'*I* don't,' said Sam, 'and it's a hyacinth, actually – very nourishing. Trouble with you is – you don't recognize good food when you see it. Now, only a hundred years ago, the boys at Radley College

used to dig up cowslip roots and crocuses – and hyacinth bulbs from the garden. The gardeners used to go round the bend – no flowers.'

'But why?' asked Minty.

' 'Cos they never got enough to eat. Collected acorns, too, and roasted them in the dormitories by candle-flame. Those were the days.'

'Were they really hungry, then?'

' 'Course they were. And very good for kids, too. Teach them not to expect too much and get uppity. People have been sending their kids away from home for centuries, to rough it. Why, back in the 1400s, they used to do it. The rich, that is. Sent their children to other people's, and vice versa. Found other people's children did more work around the house. Excellent idea. And then, they saved on meals, too – gave the other kids coarse bread and beer and cold meat every day.'

'What a rotten thing to do,' said Minty.

'Sensible, though. Depends how you look at it. Now, the Victorians weren't softies, either, giving children all the best things. If you indulged yourself in a wicked thing like a lollipop, then you were for it. There'd be a dose of rhubarb and salt waiting for you, just to teach you a lesson.'

'But surely their own children had good food, if they could afford it?'

'Well, take Augustus Hare. He was a little boy, about six. He had mutton and rice pudding for dinner every single day. Nothing unusual in that – it was kids' food. Now one day, his family started talking at dinner about all kinds of delicious puddings. Things Augustus had never heard of or seen before. His mouth began to water. He got really hopeful. Well, the great moment arrived. The puddings were actually brought in, and put on the table.'

'What were they?' asked Minty.

'Hedgehogs of sponge-cake, spiked with almonds, snowy creams covered with macaroons and candied fruits, apple pies, crustings of icing and big red cherries, smooth apricot creams, trembling jellies . . .'

'Coo, lucky thing,' said Minty.

'That's what Augustus thought,' went on Sam. 'Until his mother told him to get up at once and take them down to the poor people in the village. That's called character-building. Or mental cruelty. Or good manners.'

'Well, I'm glad it's different now,' said Minty. Still, she put back her third biscuit.

'It takes all sorts,' said Sam. 'Now, in Siberia, you, being a woman, would have to skin the reindeer for dinner, cut it up, cook it, and then if you were lucky you'd get the leftover bones at the end of the meal. They've got a saying there: "Being woman, eat crumbs".'

'But women are supposed to be served first.'

'Depends where you are,' said Sam. 'Not in Mexico you wouldn't be, either. You wait till the end and lump it!'

He poured himself another cup of tea. Minty noticed he didn't offer her one.

'It's not that I'm *expecting* anything, or feeling *uppity*,' she said. 'But do you think I could have a cup?'

Sam looked up in surprise. 'If you're a sorcerer, you can have a cuppa to go with it. *I* don't see a cup anywhere.' It was true. He had the only one. 'Still,' he went on, patting himself all over. 'I *am* a wizard in my spare time,' and he proceeded to take three white cups and a blue mug out of his inside pockets. 'Help yourself.'

What's for dinner? What's for dinner?
  Irish spew, Irish spew,
   Sloppy semolina, sloppy semolina.
No thank you! No thank you!

Table manners

I eat my peas with honey,
I've done it all my life,
It makes the peas taste funny,
But it keeps them on the knife.

Some people (not mentioning any names) do go on about table manners. 'Sit up straight. Don't put your elbows on the table. Use your fork, for goodness sake', etc, etc. Of course, parents always behaved perfectly when they were young, but before that, things were *much* worse.

In about 1290, an Italian friar wrote the 'Fifty Courtesies of the Table'. Some of them were: Don't mention any flies or dirt you see in the food; Don't wipe your mouth with your hand after drinking; Don't start fights at the table.

Training a Child to Avoid Greed

In 1440, people were told: Don't claw your back as if after a flea, or your head as if after a louse. (Not at mealtimes, anyway – let it bite you and you can have a good scratch afterwards.)

Until the seventeenth century, not many people used forks, so eating was a sticky business. Poor Charles II had lunch with Louis XIV one day. They used a knife and fingers. Now, King Charles was very polite and well brought up, so every time he spoke to Louis's wife at lunch, he raised his hat to her. (Why he wore his hat at lunch is another matter.) By the end of the meal, his hat was just a greasy old rag . . .

('God in His wisdom has provided man with natural forks. It is considered impious to substitute them by metallic articles when eating.')

Then there was all that throwing about of food at banquets . . .

Don't – said a Book of Demeanour – pick your nose, or blow it on the tablecloth! Don't prowl around your head searching for lice!

George Washington wrote a book about behaviour when he was *only fourteen*. There were about a hundred rules. Rule ninety-five: Don't put your meat in your mouth with your knife, or spit out stones from fruit pies, or throw food under the table.

Crazy cookery

To make Gosky Patties, by Edward Lear

Take a pig, three or four years of age, and tie him by the off-hind leg to a post. Place five pounds of currants, three of sugar, two pecks of peas, eighteen roast chestnuts, a candle and six bushels of turnips within his reach; if he eats these, constantly provide him with more.

Then procure some cream, some slices of Cheshire cheese, four quires of foolscap paper and a packet of black pins. Work the whole into a paste, and spread it out to dry on a sheet of clean brown waterproof linen.

When the paste is perfectly dry, but not before, proceed to beat the pig violently with the handle of a large broom. If he squeals, beat him again.

Visit the paste and beat the pig alternately for some days, and ascertain if at the end of that period the whole is about to turn into Gosky Patties.

If it does not then, it never will; in that case the pig may be let loose, and the whole process may be considered as finished.

An improved dinner-wagon

Answers

Guess when? on page 20

This was taking place 1,800 years ago in Italy.

Guess what? on page 21

1 Sausage
2 Champagne
3 Cake
4 Cheese
5 Sauce
6 Artichokes
7 Oranges (for marmalade)
8 Wine
9 Buns
10 Rock
11 Cheese
12 Port (wine)
13 An ice-cream cake ('Baked Alaska')
14 Cakes
15 Cheese
16 Lamb, and butter and cheese
17 Beef ('Aberdeen Angus' is a kind of cattle)
18 Sprouts

A hard day's night on page 52

This is rhyming slang:

carving-knife = wife
butcher's (hook) = look
mince-pies = eyes
bees and honey = money
elephant's trunk = drunk
Irish stew = true
loaf of bread = head
rabbit and pork = talk
apples and pears = stairs
bacon and eggs = legs

plates (of meat) = feet
quaker oat = coat
this and that = hat
Dicky dirt = shirt
pot and pan = man
fife and drum = bum
Noah's ark = dark
round the houses = trousers
Uncle Ned = bed

Who said? on page 74

1 Napoleon
2 Marie Antoinette
3 Charles Dickens
4 William Shakespeare (*King Lear*)
5 The man in the wilderness
6 Simple Simon

Who was it? on page 74

1 The owl and the pussy-cat
2 The Queen
3 The Queen of Hearts
4 Jack Sprat and his wife
5 Little Jack Horner
6 Little Tommy Tucker
7 King Alfred
8 Taffy the Welshman
9 Tom Kitten
10 John the Baptist

Call my bluff on page 129

Cous-cous are millet flour dumplings.
Mishmish is a kind of Middle Eastern apricot.
Camu-camu is a fruit which grows in the Amazon Basin.
The pawpaw is the fruit of a South American tree.

Odd man out on page 130

1 Botticelli is the odd man out. He was an Italian painter. (Broccoli is a green vegetable, and the others are different kinds of Italian pasta.)
2 Giorgione is the odd man out – he too was an Italian painter.
3 Anne is the odd woman out. ('Apple Charlotte' is a pudding; 'Johnny cake' is a bun; 'Chicken Véronique' is chicken with a white wine sauce and grapes; 'Peach Melba' is ice-cream and a peach covered in raspberry sauce, named after Dame Nellie Melba, the singer; 'Baba' is a small cake, often soaked in rum and called *baba au rhum*; rosemary is a bush, the leaves of which are used to flavour foods.)
4 Banter
5 Teazle

6 Flutter. (A fritter is a food dipped in batter and fried; flummery is a dish of sugar, cream, sherry and oatmeal; frumenty is an old dish of soaked and cooked wheat; flounder is a fish; fricassée is cooked meat warmed up in white sauce.)

What are they? on page 143

1 Mangelwurzel is a kind of beet fed to cattle.
2 Horseradish is the root of a plant; it's usually grated and mixed with cream to make a sauce. It has a hot taste and is eaten with beef.
3 A samovar is a Russian tea-urn.
4 Sweetbreads are the pancreas of an animal.
5 A shish-kebab is a Turkish dish in which small pieces of meat and vegetables are put on a skewer and grilled.
6 A kedgeree is a dish of rice mixed with fish.
7 Arrowroot is a starch which comes from the rhizomes of a plant. It's used to thicken clear sauces.
8 A skillet is a cooking pot, like a frying pan.
9 Dill is a herb.
10 Yeast is a living fungus, used to make bread dough rise, and in making beer.
11 A roll-mop is a boned herring, pickled in vinegar and rolled round a piece of onion.
12 A rissole is a round ball of cooked meat, fried.
13 A soufflé is a dish made of egg-yolks and whipped whites, which is light and frothy.
14 A colander is a metal or plastic bowl with holes in it, to drain food in.
15 Guava is the fruit of a tropical American tree.
16 A kipper is a smoked herring.

True or false? on page 143

1 Not entirely true – but carrots do help your eyes to adapt from light to dark more efficiently.
2 False

3 False. Milk is not a complete food, though you could certainly keep alive on it for quite a while.

4 False. No *one* food makes you strong. But spinach does contain many useful minerals.

5 Almost true. You *could* eat them in other months, but it's not a good idea.

6 True. The green part can give you solanine poisoning. (They go green when exposed to sunlight.)

7 False

8 False

9 True. Lots of vegetables do lose valuable vitamins when they are cooked.

10 False

Grisslegrease Grammar School Menu on page 144

Pig swill = dinner
Irish spew = Irish stew
Bilge = gravy
Garbage = cabbage
Door steps = hunks of bread
Resurrection pie = shepherd's pie
Seaweed = greens
Cannonballs = peas

Armoured cow = corned beef
Worms = spaghetti
Rabbit's food = salad
Frog's spawn or snottie gog pie
    = tapioca
Stodge = suet pudding with jam
Brylcreem = white sauce

Acknowledgements

I would like to thank the following for permission to include copyright material:

Gerald Duckworth & Co Ltd, for four illustrations from *Inventions* by Heath Robinson; André Deutsch Ltd, for recipes by Sir John Betjeman, Spike Milligan, Tommy Steele and Sir Edmund Hillary from *Celebrity Cooking*, edited by Renée Hellman; *Punch* for four 'recipes'.

I am very grateful to lots of people who gave me information for this book. I would particularly like to thank Mr G. L. Whislay of the Ministry of Agriculture, Fisheries and Food, for sending me ration books and a great many useful facts about food rationing; Arabella Boxer, for information about the Jains; the Editor of the *Fish Friers' Review*; the office of the Lord Mayor of London; Dr Patrick Hamilton, Jocasta Innes and Mrs Eve Turner.

The most useful book I read, which told me a great deal about the composition of foods, the discovery of vitamins and the history of nutrition, is *The Foundations of Nutrition* by Clara Mae Taylor and Orrea Florence Pye. *The Composition of Foods* by R. A. McCance and E. M. Widdowson was also of great help to me. And Frederick J. Simmoons' book, *Eat Not This Flesh*, gave me many instances of food avoidance and food habits around the world.

Other books I read in preparation for this book are:

Technological Eating Dr Magnus Pyke
Food and Society Dr Magnus Pyke
La Cuisine des Pauvres Robert Morel (Ed)
Earth Medicine, Earth Foods Michael A. Weiner
Good Things in England Florence White (Ed)
English Eccentrics Edith Sitwell
Food Customs Don Lewis
Consuming Passions Philippa Pullar
A Baronial Household of the 13th Century Margaret Wade Labarge
Frying Tonight: A Saga of Fish and Chips Gerald Priestland
The Pleasure of Your Company Jean Latham
Movable Feasts Arnold Palmer
The Lonely Sea and the Sky Francis Chichester
The Cornflake Crusade G. Carson

Newspapers and magazines have been useful sources for facts, too, especially the LOOK column of the *Sunday Times*, which investigated the components of many ordinary foods; also *The Times*, the *Daily Mirror*, the *New Yorker*, *Nature*, the *Listener*, the *Countryman*, *Look and Learn* and *World of Wonder*.

Fun with Piccolo

Piccolo Book of Riddles (illus) 30p
S. B. Cunningham

A bumper book of riddles from around the world. All the old chestnuts are included as well as a lot of new ones.

Piccolo Book of Jokes (illus) 30p
Margaret Grosset

Q. When is an operation funny?
A. When it leaves the patient in stitches.
There's a groan a minute in this collection of jokes, puns, and riddles.

Tomfoolery (illus) 30p
Alvin Schwartz

Tricks with words to trip you up and muddle your friends.

Witcracks (illus) 30p
Alvin Schwartz

Jokes of all sorts: riddles, puns, ancient jokes, modern jokes, shaggy dog stories, even 'Confucius say' jokes.

Nut-crackers (illus) 20p
John Jaworski and Ian Stewart

Puzzles and games to boggle the mind! You'll find all manner of things to do, things to make, and things to look at in this entertaining book – word games, string puzzles, mazes, codes, number patterns, skeleton crosswords – and not forgetting Professor Crankshaft's Impossible Objects!

Piccolo non-fiction

Piccolo Cook Book   (illus) 25p
Second Piccolo Cook Book (illus) 25p

Marguerite Patten

If you enjoy cooking you should read these two books from this
well-known cookery writer.

They have been written especially for all young cooks, so that you
can delight and surprise your friends and family with delicious dishes
and even whole meals.

Both books are jam-packed with step-by-step instructions, advice
on utensils needed and practical recipes which are simple to follow
and fun to prepare.

You can buy these and other Piccolo books from booksellers and
newsagents; or direct from the following address:
Pan Books, Cavaye Place, London SW10 9PG
Send purchase price plus 15p for the first book and 5p for
each additional book, to allow for postage and packing

While every effort is made to keep prices low, it is sometimes
necessary to increase prices at short notice. Pan Books reserve the
right to show on covers new retail prices which may differ
from those advertised in the text or elsewhere